Investment Appraisal
and
Financing Decisions

Students' Manual

The Chapman & Hall Series in Accounting and Finance

Consulting editors
John Perrin, Emeritus Professor of the University of Warwick and Price
Waterhouse Fellow in Public Sector Accounting at the University of Exeter;
Richard M.S. Wilson, Professor of Management Control in the School of Finance
and Information at the Queen's University of Belfast and L.C.L. Skerratt, Professor
of Financial Accounting at the University of Manchester.

H.M. Coombs and D.E. Jenkins
Public Sector Financial Management

J.C. Drury
Management and Cost Accounting (2nd edn)
(Also available: **Students' Manual, Teachers' Manual**)

C.R. Emmanuel, D.T. Otley and K. Merchant
Accounting for Management Control (2nd edn)
(Also available: **Teachers' Manual**)

C.R. Emmanuel, D.T. Otley and K. Merchant (editors)
Readings in Accounting for Management Control

D. Henley, C. Holtham, A. Likierman and J. Perrin
Public Sector Accounting and Financial Control (3rd edn)

R.C. Laughlin and R.H. Gray
Financial Accounting: method and meaning
(Also available: **Teachers' Guide**)

G.A. Lee
Modern Financial Accounting (4th edn)
(Also available: **Solutions Manual**)

T.A. Lee
Income and Value Measurement (3rd edn)

T.A. Lee
Company Financial Reporting (2nd edn)

T.A. Lee
Cash Flow Accounting

S.P. Lumby
Investment Appraisal and Financing Decisions (4th edn)
(Also available: **Students' Manual**)

A.G. Puxty and J.C. Dodds
Financial Management: method and meaning (2nd edn)
(Also available: **Teachers' Guide**)

J.M. Samuels, F.M. Wilkes and R.E. Brayshaw
Management of Company Finance (5th edn)
(Also available: **Students' Manual**)

B.C. Williams and B.J. Spaul
IT and Accounting: the impact of information technology

R.M.S. Wilson and Wai Fong Chua
Managerial Accounting: method and meaning
(Also available: **Teachers' Guide**)

Investment Appraisal and Financing Decisions

FOURTH EDITION

STUDENTS' MANUAL

Stephen Lumby

CHAPMAN & HALL
University and Professional Division
London · New York · Tokyo · Melbourne · Madras

UK	Chapman & Hall, 2–6 Boundary Row, London SE1 8HN
USA	Chapman & Hall, 29 West 35th Street, New York NY10001
JAPAN	Chapman & Hall Japan, Thomson Publishing Japan, Hirakawacho Nemoto Building, 7F, 1-7-11 Hirakawa-cho, Chiyoda-ku, Tokyo 102
AUSTRALIA	Chapman & Hall Australia, Thomas Nelson Australia, 102 Dodds Street, South Melbourne, Victoria 3205
INDIA	Chapman & Hall India, R. Seshadri, 32 Second Main Road, CIT East, Madras 600 035

First edition 1991

© 1991 The Lumby Family Partnership

Typeset in 10.5/11pt Times by Graphicraft Typesetters, Hong Kong
Printed in Great Britain by Page Bros. (Norwich) Ltd

ISBN 0 412 41480 5

British Library Cataloguing in Publication Data
Lumby, Stephen
   Investment appraisal and financing decisions:
   Students' manual. – (Chapman & Hall series in
   accounting and finance)
   I. Title II. Series
   332.6
   ISBN 0–412–41480–5

Library of Congress Cataloging-in-Publication Data
Available

Contents

Preface		viii
1	**Introduction**	1
	Answer to problem 1	1
	Answer to problem 2	2
2	**Traditional methods of investment appraisal**	3
	Answer to problem 1	3
	Answer to problem 2	4
3	**The single-period investment-consumption decision model**	7
	Answer to problem 1	7
4	**The discounted cash flow approach**	10
	Answer to problem 1	10
	Answer to problem 2	13
	Answer to problem 3	15
5	**Net present value and internal rate of return**	17
	Answer to problem 1	17
	Answer to problem 2	18
	Answer to problem 3	21
	Answer to problem 4	24
6	**Project appraisal cash flows**	26
	Answer to problem 1	26
	Answer to problem 2	27
	Answer to problem 3	29
7	**Capital market imperfections**	33
	Answer to problem 1	33
	Answer to problem 2	34
	Answer to problem 3	36
8	**Risk and expected return**	40
	Answer to problem 1	40

9   Portfolio theory   43
     Answer to problem 1   43
     Answer to problem 2   45
     Answer to problem 3   49

10 The capital asset pricing model   50
     Answer to problem 1   50
     Answer to problem 2   52
     Answer to problem 3   54
     Answer to problem 4   55

11 Traditional approaches to risk   59
     Answer to problem 1   59
     Answer to problem 2   63
     Answer to problem 3   67
     Answer to problem 4   69

12 The cost of company capital   72
     Answer to problem 1   72
     Answer to problem 2   74
     Answer to problem 3   77

13 The weighted average cost of capital   79
     Answer to problem 1   79
     Answer to problem 2   81
     Answer to problem 3   84
     Answer to problem 4   85

14 The capital structure decision in a no-tax world   89
     Answer to problem 1   89
     Answer to problem 2   90
     Answer to problem 3   91

15 Capital structure in a world with tax   94
     Answer to problem 1   94
     Answer to problem 2   97
     Answer to problem 3   101

16 The capital structure decision in practice   104
     Answer to problem 1   104
     Answer to problem 2   107

17 Investment and financing decision interactions   111
     Answer to problem 1   111
     Answer to problem 2   112
     Answer to problem 3   114

18 Overseas capital investments   118
     Answer to problem 1   118
     Answer to problem 2   121
     Answer to problem 3   125
     Answer to problem 4   127

19 The dividend decision   130
     Answer to problem 1   130
     Answer to problem 2   133
     Answer to problem 3   135

Preface

This *Students' Manual* provides clear and detailed solutions to the questions found at the end of each chapter of the fourth edition of *Investment Appraisal and Financing Decisions*. I would like to take the opportunity provided by this Preface to suggest the way in which this Manual might by used.

First of all, it should not be used simply as a means of 'auditing' the answers, without first attempting the questions. Although this type of use is not a complete waste of time, it is by no means an efficient use either of the questions themselves, or of these solutions.

Ideally, what the reader should do is to study the appropriate chapter in the textbook carefully and thoughtfully in order to try and gain a real *understanding* of the subject matter – the 'why' as well as the 'how'. In the textbook I have gone to great lengths to try and explain things more simply and clearly than is found in most other Financial Management texts, purely to help the reader towards a genuine understanding.

The end-of-chapter questions should then be seen as a test of your level of understanding. Have a go at them in two stages. The first stage is to attempt to answer the questions *on your own*, without the aid of the textbook chapters or your own notes. Try and do as much as you can, as well as you can. Don't bother about how long it takes you to answer a particular question, you can always speed up in future – *once* you know how to tackle the topic covered. For the moment, your objective is not speed, but *correctness*.

Having completed the first stage as best you can, I would then suggest you go back through the questions, with your answer, but this time with the help of the appropriate textbook chapters and/or your notes. In this second stage, you should try to improve upon your existing answer – you may like to write in these improvements in a different coloured ink so as to distinguish them from your original efforts.

At the end of the second stage you should have before you what you feel is the best answer that you can manage at this stage of your studies. You can now turn to the solution in this *Students' Manual* and go through your answer slowly and carefully, noting which parts of your answer are correct and which parts are incorrect or incomplete. Pay particular attention to what you got *wrong*, not what you got right. The purpose of the Manual is to try to help you *improve* in the future, and not just to give you a 'pat on the back' in congratulations!

In the third stage, use the answers in the *Students' Manual* as a tutorial helping you to produce an even better answer.

Finally, great care has been taken to try and ensure that all errors – typesetting and otherwise – have been eliminated from the suggested solutions. However, to achieve a 100% success rate is almost impossible. Therefore, if you do find any mistakes, please accept my apologies and I would be grateful if you could write and give details. They can then be removed at the next printing and, in that way, you will have the satisfaction of knowing that future readers will not have to face the same mistakes as you did!

Many thanks and good luck with your studies – I hope that you enjoy them!

Steve Lumby

1
Introduction

Answer to problem 1

In a commercial organization, the objective of financial management decision making is to maximize shareholder wealth. In other words, the objective is to maximize the wealth of its owners.

In very simplistic terms, this can be achieved by maximizing the revenues that the firm generates and minimizing the costs of generating those revenues. Economics (in a static analysis) indicates that the optimal output point for a firm is where this difference between costs and revenues (i.e. 'profit') is maximized. In a more dynamic analysis, taking the time dimension into account, this leads on to the maximization of the worth of the company, and so the maximization of shareholder wealth.

In many ways, the objectives of financial management in a non-commercial organization such as a hospital or a charity – or perhaps a department of Government – involves much the same considerations. A non-commercial organization can be defined as one which does not *sell* its output. It is this feature that causes a problem for its financial managers, because they have difficulty in measuring their output.

However, the objective of the financial managers of non-commercial organizations remains essentially the same: maximizing the net *benefits* of their 'owners', where the owners may be society at large (as in the case of a hospital or department of Government) or to the recipients of the organization's charitable intent.

Finally, it is interesting to observe that we may well expect the same principal–agent relationship problem arising in non-commercial organizations as that arising in commercial organizations, and therefore necessitating the need for control mechanisms. Thus, given that we might assume that charities are in a competitive market for donations, one charity might try to demonstrate the equivalent of its 'shareholder wealth maximizing behaviour' against its competitors on their comparative efficiency in terms of 'administration costs per pound of donations' relative to their competition.

1

Answer to problem 2

If shareholders want to ensure that their managers act in the best interests of shareholders, then it is vital that an attempt is made to bring managers' own personal objectives in line with their shareholders' objectives. This can be done through a variety of schemes designed to give the management an incentive to be wealth maximizers rather than just satisficers.

One obvious approach would be to link management pay to profitability. This could be done either in absolute terms or in relative terms – earnings per share. However, this raises two problems. The first concerns the undoubted conflict that can occur between short-term and long-term profitability. (Problem 3 in Chapter 4 partly concerns this problem.) It is difficult to devise an incentive scheme based on long-term profitability – managers are often in their position for a relatively short term and want to be rewarded via an incentive scheme on a yearly basis – and therefore there is always the temptation to sacrifice long-term profitability for short-term profitability. (An example would be where the use of lower-quality raw materials increases product contribution, but damages the longer-term reputation of the product.)

The second difficulty with incentive schemes based on profit is that the level of profitability is not solely a function of managerial ability and effort. A large number of external macro-economic factors which are outside the control of the management – such as the rate of national economic growth – affect the profitability of the firm. A fundamental principle of any incentive scheme is that it should be related *directly* to effort and should not be affected by other factors. Thus, to reward management for a rise in profitability that is unconnected with their efforts – or to penalize them for a fall in profitability which has been caused by external economic influences outside their control – would mean that the incentive scheme was not performing its intended task.

To aviod both these problems, it would be better to link the incentive scheme to the share price of the company (or, in the case of a company whose shares are not valued on a stock market, link the incentive scheme to a periodic private valuation of the shares). In so doing, this gets over the problem of a possible conflict between the long and short term (to some extent) as the share price should reflect *all* the implications of management's actions.

In addition, if the incentive scheme was linked to *relative* share price performance, this would then ensure that only the superior or inferior actions of the management's performance would be rewarded or penalized. What is meant by linking the incentive scheme to relative share price performance, is that the link should be between the performance (i.e. increase or decrease) in the company's share price relative to the share price of its competitors. In this way macro-economic influences on the company's share price (which are largely out of the control of the management) can be 'screened out' of the incentive reward system.

2
Traditional methods of investment appraisal

Answer to problem 1

(a) *Electronics Project*
Given that the total outlay is £2m, the project pays back a total of £1.6m at Year 3 and £2.4m at Year 4. Therefore, break-even is achieved at approximately Year 3.5. The decision advice here is ambiguous. On the one hand the project does *not* pay back within three years of the project's starting date, while on the other hand it does pay back within three years (actually, 2.5 years) of the completion of the capital expenditure.

Property Project
The Property project has a straight three-year payback and so just meets the decision criterion.

Mining Project
Again, the decision advice is ambiguous. The project pays back its outlay in two years and so, on that criterion, is acceptable. However, a further outlay is required at Year 4.

(b) The best choice here is not clear. One interpretation would be to accept the Electronics project as it pays back in 2.5 years as opposed to three years for the Property project.
An alternative interpretation would be that the Property project pays back by Year 3 while the Electronics project pays back by Year 3.5. Therefore, the former should be accepted.
A further factor to consider is the post-payback cash flows. Post-payback, the Electronics project generates a further £1.2m. The Property project only generates a further £400,000 post-payback. Quite simply, there is no clearly correct decision using payback.

(c) The Mining project, on one basis, has a payback of two years against a payback of three years for the Property project. However, the Mining project requires an extra £0.75m outlay and only

3

generates a net £0.05m post-payback. In contrast, the Property project does not require any further capital expenditure and generates £0.4m post-payback. Again the correct decision advice is unclear.

(d)   The payback decision criterion should really take the project *risk* into account. The more risky the project – that is, the more uncertain its expected future cash flows – the shorter should be the maximum permitted payback.

Almost certainly, these three projects are of unequal risk. Clearly the Property project, with its rent-paying tenant already installed, has much less uncertain cash flows than the other two projects. Thus the company's use of the same decision criterion for all three divisions does not appear sensible.

Answer to problem 2

(a)   *Payback calculation* (excluding working capital)

Year	Net cash flow
0	(200,000)
1	50,000
2	60,000
3	110,000
4	{ 20,000
	{ 80,000 Scrap value

Therefore the project has less than a three-year payback and is acceptable. However, it is debatable whether, in this example, working capital (W.C.) should be excluded from the analysis as it is not fully recovered. If it were to be included, then the analysis would be:

Year	Net cash flow
0	{ (200,000)
	{ (50,000)
1	50,000
2	60,000
3	110,000
4	{ 20,000
	{ 80,000 Scrap value
	{ 40,000 Working capital recovery

The project now takes longer than three years to pay back and should *not* be accepted.

ROCE calculation
Annual depreciation: $(200,000 - 80,000) \div 4 = \underline{30,000}$

Year	Net cash flow	–	Depreciation	=	'Profit'
1	50,000	–	30,000	=	20,000
2	60,000	–	30,000	=	30,000
3	110,000	–	30,000	=	80,000
4	20,000	–	30,000	=	(10,000)
			Total profit	=	120,000

Average annual profit = 120,000 ÷ 4 = 30,000

Return on initial capital employed: $\dfrac{30,000}{250,000} = 0.12$

As the project only has a ROCE of 12%, against a decision criterion of 13%, it is unacceptable.

Advice
The project does *not* meet the firm's ROCE criterion and, on one interpretation, nor does it reach the payback criterion. Therefore, on balance, the advice would be to reject.

(b) Normally, working capital is excluded from the payback analysis on the basis that it is automatically paid back *whenever* the project is terminated: the stocks are eliminated and the debtors pay. However, in the project presently under consideration, working capital is *not* fully recovered. In such circumstances there is a strong argument for including working capital expenditure (i.e. expenditure on *current* assets) along with expenditure on fixed assets (capital expenditure) in the payback calculation.

(c) In many ways, the return on *average* capital employed is a more sensible measure of profitability than the return on initial capital employed. *Average* annual profits are compared to the *average* capital employed in generating those profits. The average annual profit is £30,000. The average capital employed is given by

$$\frac{\begin{bmatrix} \text{Capital expenditure} \\ + \\ \text{W.C. expenditure} \end{bmatrix} + \begin{bmatrix} \text{Scrap value} \\ + \\ \text{W.C. recovered} \end{bmatrix}}{2}$$

$$\frac{(200,000 + 50,000) + (80,000 + 40,000)}{2} = \text{£}185,000$$

Therefore the return on average capital employed is

$$\frac{\text{£}\,30,000}{\text{£}185,000} = 0.162 \text{ or } \underline{16.2\%}$$

On this basis, given the firm's decision criterion, the project should be accepted. I hope that I get that promotion!

(d)   There are two major drawbacks with the ROCE/ARR as an investment appraisal decision rule. One is that it ignores the time value of money. The other is that it tries to use a *reporting* concept – accounting profit – in a *decision-making* context.

In contrast, the payback technique does use a cash flow analysis of the decision, which is correct. A capital investment decision is an economic, resource-allocation decision and the economic unit of account in such circumstances is cash or cash flow. Thus, between the two appraisal techniques, payback is to be preferred, even though it too ignores the concept of the time value of money. However, this criticism can easily be overcome by using a variation on payback: Discounted Payback – see Chapter 3.

3
The single-period investment-consumption decision model

Answer to problem 1

(a) Figure 3.1 shows the physical investment line facing the firm.
(b) From the graph in (a) it can be seen that the point of tangency between the Physical Investment Line (PIL) and the Financial Investment Line (FIL) indicates the firm's investment decision.

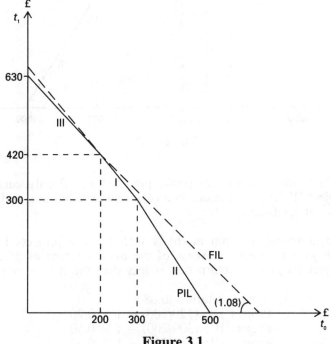

Figure 3.1

7

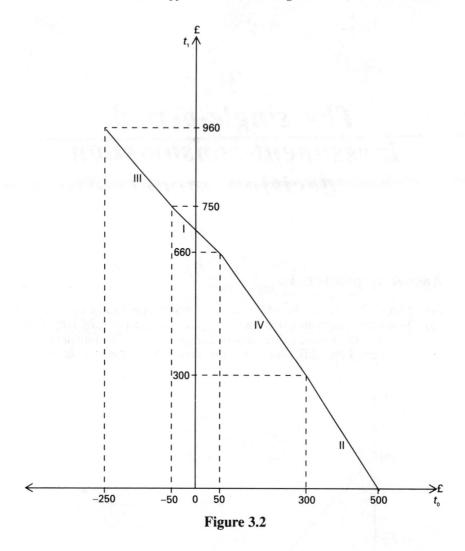

Figure 3.2

At t_0, the firm will undertake project I and II only, and reject project III. This will result in a cash flow of £200 at t_0 and a cash flow of £420 *at t_1*.

(c) The graphical decision in (b) is such because projects I and II both give a return in excess of the market return of 8%, while project III gives a return that is less than the market return:

Market return = 0.08
Project I : (120/100) − 1 = 0.20
Project II : (300/200) − 1 = 0.50
Project III: (210/200) − 1 = 0.05

    (i)   If the market interest rate moved to 4%, then all three projects would be accepted.

    (ii)   If the market interest rate moved to 25%, then only project II would be accepted.

    (iii)   If the market interest rate moved to 20%, then project II would be accepted and project III would be rejected. However, the firm would be indifferent between accepting or rejecting project I as it gives the same return as the market.

(d)   The new project produces a return of 32% $[(330/250) - 1 = 0.32]$. Thus the firm would now undertake projects I, II and IV. However this would require a total investment of £550 at t_0. As the firm only has £500 available at t_0, it should borrow the additional £50 required at the market interest rate of 8%.

     If the firm cannot borrow additional resources, or does not wish to do so, then the optimal investment decision is to accept projects II and IV and 50% of project I, as Figures 3.2 shows.

4
The discounted cash flow approach

Answer to problem 1

(a) *NPV calculation (£m)*

Year	Capital expenditure	Net Revenue
0	−1.8	+0.5
1		
.		.
.		.
.		.
.		.
6		+0.5
7		+0.3
.		.
.		.
10	+0.5	+0.3

$-1.8 + 0.5\ A_{\overline{6}|0.18} + 0.3\ A_{\overline{4}|0.18}\ (1.18)^{-6} + 0.5\ (1.18)^{-10}$

$-1.8 + (0.5 \times 3.4976) + (0.3 \times 2.6901 \times 0.3704) + (0.5 \times 0.1911)$

$-1.8 + 1.7488 + 0.2989 + 0.0955 = +$ <u>£343,200</u> NPV.

(b) *ROCE calculation (£m)*

Depreciation: $(1.8 - 0.5) \div 10 = $ £0.13m/year

Annual profit: $0.5 - 0.13 = $ £0.37m/year, Years 1 to 6
$0.3 - 0.13 = $ £0.17m/year, Years 7 to 10

Average annual profit: $[(0.37 \times 6) + (0.17 \times 4)] \div 10 = $ <u>£0.29m</u>

Average capital employed: $\dfrac{1.8 + 0.5}{2} = $ <u>£1.15m</u>

10

$$\text{Return on average capital employed} = \frac{0.29}{1.15} = 0.252 \text{ or } \underline{25.2\%}$$

$$\text{Return on initial capital employed} = \frac{0.29}{1.8} = 0.161 \text{ or } \underline{16.1\%}$$

(c) The project pays back its outlay on capital expenditure after 3.6 years.

(d) *Report to the Chairman*
Trionym PLC

Subject: Chocolate-coating machine decision

It is advised that the capital expenditure proposal should be evaluated on the basis of the net present value (NPV) decision rule. This decision rule, given certain assumptions which are outlined below, will ensure that projects are selected only if they lead to an increase in the market value of the company's shares.

On this basis, the chocolate-coating machine presently under consideration should be undertaken as it has a positive NPV of £343,200. This indicates that, as a result of acceptance, the total market value of Trionym's equity should rise by this amount (and so increase shareholders' wealth).

The NPV investment appraisal decision rule can be justified on the basis of a number of interconnected reasons. Firstly, it evaluates investment proposals on the basis of cash flow, rather than profitability. This is important because a capital investment decision is an *economic* (or resource allocation) decision and the economic unit of account is *cash*, not accounting profit. This is because it is *cash*, not profit, which gives power to command resources. Accounting profit is not, in fact, a decision making concept at all. It is a *reporting* concept, used to report on the *outcome* of investment (and other) decisions.

The second reason to justify the use of NPV is that it takes account of the 'time value' or 'opportunity cost' of cash through the discounting process. Money has got a time value in the sense that a rate of interest or rate of return can be earned by investing money (the return expected from such an investment being determined by the risk involved). Therefore, when money is invested in a particular project, the opportunity cost or the rate of return available elsewhere from a similar risk investment which is foregone must be taken into account.

This is achieved through the discounting process used by the NPV technique. As a result, the magnitude of the NPV indicates how much *extra* return that particular project produces (in current terms) over and above the return available elsewhere from a similar risk investment. Therefore, by having a £343,200 positive NPV, when discounted at 18%, the chocolate-coating machine can be said to produce an extra return of that amount, over and above the 18% return available elsewhere.

This leads directly on to the third justification for the use of the

NPV decision rule. The magnitude of the NPV indicates the increase in the company's total equity market value – or the increase in shareholder wealth – that will arise from the project. Thus the decision rule can be seen to link in directly with the company's overall objective.

However, there are two important reservations that should be mentioned about the advice given above. The first is that it is assumed that the company is not facing any form of *effective* capital expenditure constraint (either internally or externally imposed). The second is that an 18% discount rate does correctly reflect the project's risk and so represents the return available elsewhere on the capital market from an investment with a similar degree of risk.

(e)

£ms

Year	Capital expenditure	Net cash flow		18% discount		Present value cash flow
0	−1.8		×	1.0	=	−1.8
1		+0.5	×	0.8475	=	+0.4237
2		+0.5	×	0.7182	=	+0.3591
3		+0.5	×	0.6086	=	+0.3043
4		+0.5	×	0.5158	=	+0.2579
5		+0.5	×	0.4371	=	+0.2185
6		+0.5	×	0.3704	=	+0.1852
7		+0.3	×	0.3139	=	+0.0942
.		.				.
.		.				.

Discounted payback: 6.5 years (approx.)

Memo to the Chairman: Discounted payback

(i)   Discounted payback is a 'truncated' version of NPV. In other words, instead of calculating a project's NPV over the whole of its expected life, an artificial time horizon (or cut-off point) is applied: the maximum acceptable payback time period. Under these circumstances, the project is undertaken only if it manages to produce *at least* a zero NPV by the cut-off point.

(ii) In the case of the chocolate-coating machine, given a five-year payback criterion, the project will not produce a positive NPV at the end of five years: only after 6.5 years will it reach the zero NPV break-even point.

(iii) Discounted payback has all the advantages of the normal NPV technique, but with one important addition. Many companies feel that they only have a limited ability to forecast accurately future project cash flows and so are uncomfortable at making a decision on a project based on forecasted cash flows over the *whole* of its life, when some of the estimated cash flows in later years may be more like *guesses* rather than estimates. Discounted payback can be used to acknowledge this reality by placing on the project's evaluation an artificial time horizon, which may be used to indicate the perceived limits of the management's forecasting ability.

(iv) However, this additional advantage of discounted payback is also a disadvantage. The technique does not take into account project cash flows that arise outside the maximum acceptable payback criterion. Thus the decision making process may be seriously biased towards shorter-term rather than longer-term projects.

(f) The main problem with the current investment appraisal procedures of Trionym PLC is that the decision rules can give conflicting advice. Under these circumstances, it is not at all clear how the company would resolve such conflicts nor is it clear whether such a resolution would necessarily lead to optimal decisions being taken.

Answer to problem 2

(a)

		Project 1	Project 2
		£000	£000
(i)	*Accounting rate of return*		
	Cash flow	200	500
	− Depreciation (see below)	100	263
	= Average accounting profit	100	237
	Initial investment	556	1,616
	− Scrap value	56	301
	Total depreciation	500	1,315
	÷ 5		
	= Annual depreciation	100	263
	Average book value of investment		

$$\frac{556 + 56}{2} = 306$$

$$\frac{1,616 + 301}{2} = 958.5$$

		Project 1	Project 2
	Accounting rate of return	32.7%	24.7%
(ii)	*Net present value*		
Year	Initial outlay	(556)	(1,616)
1–5	200 × 3.4331	687	
	500 × 3.4331		1,717
5	Residual value		
	56 × 0.5194	29	
	301 × 0.5194		156
	Net present value	+160	+257

(iii) *Internal rate of return*

Project 1
At 14%   NPV = +160
At 20%   NPV = + 64

$$\text{IRR} = \quad 14\% + \left[\frac{160}{160 - 64}\right] \times (20\% - 14\%) = \underline{24\%}$$

Project 2
At 14%   NPV = +257
At 20%   NPV =   0
IRR =   <u>20%</u>

(iv) *Payback period*

Annual cash flows	200	500
Initial investment	556	1,616
Payback period in years	<u>2.8</u>	<u>3.2</u>

Project	*Project 1*	*Project 2*
(i) Accounting rate of return	32.7%	24.7%
(ii) Net present value (£000)	+160	+257
(iii) Internal rate of return	24%	20%
(iv) Payback period (years)	2.8	3.2

Rankings	*Best project*
(i) Accounting rate of return	1
(ii) Net present value	2
(iii) Internal rate of return	1
(iv) Payback period	1

(b) On the basis of the calculations made in answer to part (a), Congo Ltd should undertake Project 2. In doing so they would be following the advice given by the NPV decision rule and would be rejecting the advice given by the other three decision criteria.

The NPV decision advice should be accepted because it gives the correct decision advice, given a perfect capital market. Project 2 will lead to the greatest increase in shareholder wealth as it has the largest positive NPV.

All three of the other investment appraisal techniques can be faulted and so give unreliable decision advice.

(i)   The ARR evaluates the projects in percentage terms and so ignores differences in outlay. It does not use any discounting process and so ignores the time value of money. It evaluates the projects on the basis of their profitability which is incorrect. Accounting profit is a reporting concept, not a decision making concept.

(ii) The IRR method cannot be relied upon to give the correct decision advice in a situation such as this which involves mutually exclusive projects. This is for two reasons. One is because, like the ARR, it evaluates on the basis of a percentage and so ignores differences in project outlay. The other is that it employs an incorrect assumption about the rate at which project-generated cash flows are reinvested.

(iii) The payback method can be criticized on two grounds. First, as discounted payback has not been used, the time value of money has been ignored. Second, the approach does not evaluate project cash flows that lie beyond the project payback time period.

Answer to problem 3

(a) Project A: 3.32 years payback
     B: 3 years payback
     C: 2 years payback

(b) The accounting rates of return have been calculated on *initial* capital employed:

Average net cash flow: £129,140
Annual depreciation: £50,000
Average annual profit: £129,140 − £50,000 = £79,140
ARR = 79,140/350,000 = 0.2261 or 22.61%   } A

Average net cash flow: £154,000
Annual depreciation: £70,000
Average annual profit: £84,000
ARR = 84,000/350,000 = 0.24 or 24%   } B

Average net cash flow: £157,500
Annual depreciation: £87,500
Average annual profit: £70,000
ARR = 70,000/350,000 = 0.20 or 20%   } C

(c) *Supporting calculations*

	A	B	C	*Preferred*
NPV	£83,201	£64,001	£79,000	A
IRR	27.5%	26.4%	33%	C
Payback	3.32 years	3 years	2 years	C
ARR	22.61%	24%	20%	B

Your report should cover the following points.
(i)   A should be accepted if the company wishes to maximize shareholder wealth. It has the largest positive NPV.
(ii) This decision assumes a perfect capital market and that 20% correctly reflects the risk of the three projects.
(iii) This advice is at odds with the company's two normal methods (ARR and payback) as well as Stadler's IRR-backed advice.

(iv) The advice is based on the argument that (1) cash is the correct unit of account for economic/resource allocation decisions and (2) the time value of money should also be taken into account.

(v)   Payback and ARR are therefore not suitable appraisal methods. Payback ignores the time value of money (unless discounted payback is used) and ARR deals in accounting profits, not cash flows, as well as also ignoring the time value of money.

(vi) The IRR advice is also unreliable in a mutually exclusive project decision situation because it makes an incorrect assumption about the reinvestment rate of project-generated cash flows. (See the following chapter.)

(d) Stadler's choice implies that the market share price is determined by the current earnings. This is not the case. The share price is determined by future expected cash flows.

The market is only interested in current earnings if they can impart information or act as a guide as to the future cash flow. Thus Stadler is ignoring the fact that at Year 3, Project C will produce only a single further cash flow of £40,000. In contrast, Project A produces a stream of significant cash flows right up to Year 7. Hence Stadler's choice of project is unlikely to lead to maximizing the company's share price at Year 3.

5
Net present value and internal rate of return

Answer to problem 1

(a) *Type A*
    At 4% NPV = +558 (approx.)
    At 20% NPV = + 47 (approx.)

$$\text{IRR} = 4\% + \left[\frac{558}{558 - 47} \times (20\% - 4\%) \right] = \underline{21.5\%}$$

Type B
    At 4% NPV = +849 (approx.)
    At 20% NPV = − 86 (approx.)

$$\text{IRR} = 4\% + \left[\frac{849}{849 + 86} \times (20\% - 4\%) \right] = \underline{18.5\%}$$

Differential Cash Flow (A − B)
+ 1000 − 290 $A_{\overline{5}|i}$ = O NPV
At 4% NPV = −291
At 20% NPV = +133

$$\text{IRR} = 4\% + \left[\frac{-291}{-291 - 133} \times (20\% - 4\%) \right] = \underline{15.0\%}$$

The decision rule is that:
If the IRR of the differential cash flow is less than the 'hurdle rate', accept the project with the greatest IRR; and if the IRR of the differential cash flow is greater than the hurdle rate, accept the project with the smallest IRR.

    In this case, Saucy Steamboats' hurdle rate is 10%. As the IRR of the differential cash flow is 15.0% then the project with the *smallest* IRR – the Type B boat – should be accepted.

(b) There are a number of problems concerning the use of the internal rate of return decision rule for investment appraisal purposes. A problem that is common to both decisions involving single independent projects and decisions involving mutually exclusive projects is that of multiple internal rates of return. Any investment project's cash flow is likely to have multiple internal rates of return if the cash flow is of a non-standard form, i.e. where the cash flow contains more than one change of sign. As a rule of thumb, a cash flow will have as many IRRs as it has changes in sign. One particular non-standard cash flow is extremely common because of the fact that tax is chargable twelve months in arrears; *after tax* project cash flows will then typically exhibit the signs:

$$- \quad + \quad + \quad + \quad + \quad ... \quad + \quad + \quad -$$

In this cash flow there are two changes in sign and so two IRRs can be expected. The problem is that in such circumstances, the IRR decisions rules break down absolutely and cannot be operated reliably.

Another serious problem with the IRR is confined to decisions concerning mutually exclusive projects. Under these circumstances the 'normal' IRR decision rule, i.e. accept whichever alternative project produces the largest IRR (given that it exceeds the cut-off rate), cannot be relied upon to give the correct investment decision advice. The problem is caused by the fact that the IRR calculation for a project implicitly assumes that the project cash flows possess an opportunity cost equal to the IRR of the generating project. Thus, when comparing mutually exclusive projects with different IRRs, the implicit assumption becomes inconsistent and, as a result, the decision rule fails. A modified decision rule can be used (as in (a) above) but the whole is really no more than a rule of thumb with very little underlying logic to sustain it.

In contrast, given the circumstances surrounding Saucy Steamboats Ltd, the net present value decision rule evades these difficulties and can be relied upon to produce correct investment decision advice, given the assumption that the discount rate used reflects the project's risk level correctly.

Answer to problem 2

(a) £000s

Project A Discount rate	NPV	Project B Discount rate	NPV
4%	+21	4%	+26
8%	+14	8%	+14
12%	+ 7	12%	+ 3
18%	− 2	18%	−10

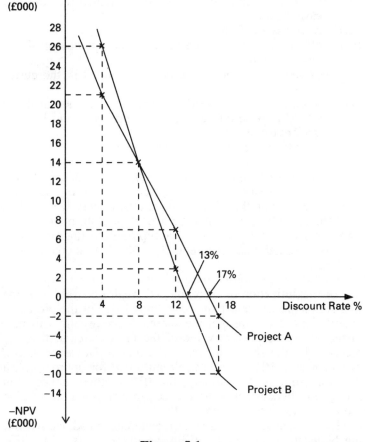

Figure 5.1

(b)   From the graph shown in Figure 5.1, the internal rate of return of Project A is approximately 17% and the internal rate of return of Project B is approximately 13%.

(c)   Based on the information given and the graph, the following advice should be given to Mr Cowdrey:
  (i)   if his discount rate is 6%, Project B should be undertaken, because at a 6% discount rate the NPV of Project B is higher than for Project A;
  (ii)   if his discount rate is 12%, Project A should be chosen, because the NPV of Project A is higher than the NPV for Project B.

(d)   The following additional information would be useful to Mr Cowdrey in making the decision:

(i)   the degree of accuracy of the cash-flow estimates

(ii)   tax implications and how these might affect the project's cash flows

(iii)   riskiness of each project

(iv)   effects, if any, of each project's acceptance on the overall business risk

(v)   existence of other projects not included in the current appraisal

(vi)   more general social effects which acceptance of the project would impose on the firm, its employees and its surrounding environment

(vii)   cut-off rate required by Mr Cowdrey.

(e)   The decision rule under the NPV method is to accept all projects which yield positive NPVs when discounted at the specified discount rate. Under the IRR method, all projects whose IRRs exceed the required rate should be accepted. Both methods give the same decision advice in simple accept/reject situations. However, we have argued that, theoretically, the NPV method should be preferred.

The NPV approach is more consistent with the assumed objective of maximization of shareholders' wealth than the IRR method. In a simple accept/reject situation, knowledge of the project's NPV is sufficient to ensure that the shareholders' wealth will be maximized when the present value of the future stream of cash flows received by the shareholders is maximized. However, knowledge of a project's IRR is not in itself sufficient for optimal investment decisions, nor is it necessary; the IRR method makes economic sense only because in simple accept/reject situations it gives the same decision as the NPV method.

The two methods may give different decision advice when choosing between two mutually exclusive investments. This difference stems from the different assumptions made regarding the reinvestment rates of intermediate cash flows. The NPV approach assumes that intermediate cash flows can be reinvested at a rate of interest equivalent to that used as the discount rate. The IRR method assumes that these can be reinvested and earn a return equal to the project's IRR. Of the two, it appears that the NPV assumption is more realistic, given a perfect capital market.

When viewed in a ranking situation, the NPV approach assumes that the discount rate reflects the opportunity cost of capital. The opportunity cost concept under the IRR method is less valid because of the IRR reinvestment assumption. In fact, the actual opportunity cost of funds does not even enter into the IRR method when the method is used for ranking.

The NPV method gives an absolute measure which may be more meaningful than the average concept used in the IRR method. Also, the NPV method is generally more flexible. It can be easily adjusted to include multiple discount rates over time.

Multiple rates of return are possible under the IRR method. The presence of multiple rates of return makes interpretation difficult, and for some patterns of cash flows, under the IRR method, it may not be possible to derive a meaningful IRR at all.

All that said, however, it is often argued that the theoretical difficulties of the IRR method are outweighed by its practical advantages. For instance, being based on a rate of return concept, the method is more easily understood and accepted by business-men. It is also argued that the method obviates the decision maker from having to work out the firm's discount rate, which in itself poses a number of problems. The NPV method, on the other hand, requires the decision maker to determine the discount rate to be used from the start.

Answer to problem 3

(a) As funds are readily available at the market interest rate of 10%, you should accept all projects having a positive net present value (NPV) when discounted at 10%. Justification for the NPV rule is based on two main assumptions:
   (i)   that the company's objective is to maximize the wealth of its shareholders, as measured by the current market value of its ordinary shares;
   (ii) that the discount rate used (the company's cost of capital) reflects the return available elsewhere on similar-risk invest-ments.

If these assumptions hold, the net present value of a project measures the amount by which the wealth of a company's share-holders will change if the project is accepted (an increase if the NPV is positive and vice versa).

The NPVs of the four projects under consideration are

<table>
<tr><td></td><td style="text-align:right">NPV</td></tr>
</table>

Project 1 $-2,500 + 1,000$ $A_{\overline{3}|0.10}$
   $-2,500 + (1,000 \times 2.4869)$ $\qquad = -13$ (Reject)

Project 2 $-1,000 + 100 (1 + 0.1)^{-1} + 1,400 (1 + 0.1)^{-2}$
   $-1,000 + (100 \times 0.9091) + (1,400 \times 0.8264)$ $= +248$ (Accept)

Project 3 $-1,000 + 800 (1 + 0.1)^{-1} + 600 (1 + 0.1)^{-2}$
   $-1,000 + (800 \times 0.9091) + (600 \times 0.8264)$ $= +223$ (Accept)

Project 4 $-4,000 + 5,000 (1 + 0.1)^{-3}$
   $-4,000 + (5,000 \times 0.7513)$ $\qquad = -243$ (Reject)

(b) The decision rule would then be: accept whichever project has the largest positive NPV. This is Project 2.

The decision rule does not have to take account of (i) differing project lives or (ii) differing capital outlays because it is assumed that (i) all considerations of risk are allowed for in the discount rate and (ii) there is a perfect capital market.

(c) *Project 2*   10% discount rate NPV +248
20% discount rate NPV + 55

$$\text{IRR} = 10\% + \left[\frac{248}{248 - 55} \times (20\% - 10\%) \right] = 23\%$$

Project 3   10% discount rate NPV +223
20% discount rate NPV + 83

$$\text{IRR} = 10\% + \left[\frac{223}{223 - 83} \times (20\% - 10\%) \right] = 26\%$$

It would not be valid to use the normal IRR decision rule for mutually exclusive projects: accept whichever project has the largest IRR, given that it is greater than the cut-off rate. This is because the IRR decision rule makes an incorrect assumption concerning the opportunity cost of project-generated cash flows which makes its decision advice unreliable when faced with mutually exclusive projects.

The alternative decision rule, making use of the IRR of the differential cash flow is:
(i)   If IRR (differential cash flow) > cut-off rate, accept the project with the smallest IRR.
(ii) If IRR (differential cash flow) < cut-off rate, accept the project with the largest IRR.

Therefore:

	Project 2	Project 3	2 minus 3
	−1,000	−1,000	0
	+ 100	+ 800	−700
	+1,400	+ 600	+800
Net undiscounted cash flow	+ 500	+ 400	
IRR	23%	26%	$14\frac{1}{3}\%$
NPV$_{10\%}$	+ 248	+ 223	

(The IRR of the incremental cash flow is found by solving

$$\frac{-700}{1 + i} + \frac{800}{(1 + i)^2} = 0 \text{ NPV}$$

Multiplying each side by $(1 + i)$:

$$-700 + \frac{800}{1 + i} = 0$$

$$800 = 700 \, (1 + i)$$
$$800 - 700 = 700i$$

$$\frac{100}{700} = i = 0.143, \text{ or } 14\frac{1}{3}\%)$$

As the IRR (2 minus 3) > 10%, accept the project with the smallest IRR (Project 2) which is, of course, the project with the largest positive NPV. The result is shown graphically in Fig. 5.2.

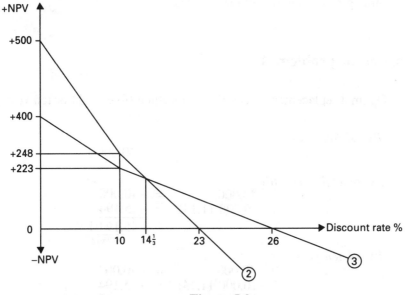

Figure 5.2

(d) The principal reasons for the managerial preference for IRR over NPV are as follows:

(i) Management are familiar with a decision rule that uses a percentage rate of return.

(ii) With IRR, the discount/cut-off rate does not have to be specified in the calculations, but only at the time of the final decision. Even then, an *exact* cut-off rate does not need to be specified. The decision can be made in reply to the question: Is this project's IRR sufficiently high to make it acceptable?

(iii) Many managements (incorrectly) see a link between a project's IRR, current market interest rates and accounting rates of return.

(iv) Many managements believe (incorrectly) that the capital rationing problem can more easily be overcome by using IRR instead of NPV (see Chapter 7).

Using IRR instead of NPV may well lead to the wrong project being selected when a mutually exclusive choice has to be made among alternatives, but it should not lead to a project being accepted that has a negative NPV (i.e. the IRR decision rule will help select investments that will increase shareholder wealth, but *not* necessarily maximize it). Of course, this ignores the problem of multiple IRRs where such a choice *is* possible, but probably unlikely. Furthermore, both DCF methods only evaluate a project in terms of their *quantifiable financial* effects. Most managements have a high level of qualitative factor inputs into a decision, e.g. strategic reasons or competitiveness.

Answer to problem 4

(i) Optimal replacement cycle of new machine (five, eight or ten years)

PV of five-year life

$$-40,000 \text{ PV}$$

PV of eight-year life

0	−40,000	=	−40,000
5	−10,000 $(1.14)^{-5}$	=	− 5,194
			−45,194 PV

PV of ten-year life

0	−40,000	=	− 40,000
5	−10,000 $(1.14)^{-5}$	=	− 5,194
8	−20,000 $(1.14)^{-8}$	=	− 7,012
			−52,206

Annual equivalent cash flows:
Five-year replacement: $-40,000 \div A_{\overline{5}|0.14} = -11,651$
Eight-year replacement: $-45,194 \div A_{\overline{8}|0.14} = - 9,742$
Ten-year replacement: $-52,206 \div A_{\overline{10}|0.14} = -10,009$

Therefore, the optimal replacement cycle of the new machine is eight years as it produces the lowest annual equivalent cash flow cost of £9,742.

(ii) Optimal replacement point of new machine (year 0, 1 or 2)

Replacement		Cash flow			
point	0	1	2	3	...
Year 0	+8000	−9742	−9742	−9742	...
Year 1	0	0	−9742	−9742	...
Year 2	0	−9000	0	−9742	...

Whenever the current machine is replaced, the cash flows from Year 3 onwards are identical. As a result, the decision can simply be based on the NPV of each set of cash flows over the next two years:

Replacement
point

Year 0:	$+8000 -9742A_{\overline{2}|0.14}$	$= -8042$ NPV
Year 1:	$-9742 \ (1.14)^{-2}$	$= -7496$ NPV
Year 2:	$-9000 \ (1.14)^{-1}$	$= -7895$ NPV

Therefore the optimal replacement point of the existing machine is in twelve month's time at Year 1. The policy results in the least-cost NPV. The new machine, as already decided, should then be replaced every eight years, *ad infinitum*.

6
Project appraisal cash flows

Answer to problem 1

In assembling the project's cash flows the following should be ignored.
(i)   *Depreciation*; this is a non-cash cost and so is irrelevant to the analysis.
(ii) *Allocated fixed overheads*; on the assumption that these represent non-incremental cash flows.
(iii) *Interest payments* (plus their associated tax relief); financing charges are *never* included in project cash flows. Instead they are implicitly reflected in the required after-tax rate of return/discount rate, which in this example is 10%.
(iv) *Dividend payments*; these too are part of the financing charges and are never explicitly included as part of a project's cash flows.

Writing down allowances

								Tax credit	Year
£1,200,000	×	0.25	=	£300,000	×	0.4	=	£120,000	1
300,000									
900,000	×	0.25	=	£225,000	×	0.4	=	£ 90,000	2
225,000									
675,000	×	0.25	=	£168,750	×	0.4	=	£ 67,500	3
168,750									
506,250	×	0.25	=	£126,562	×	0.4	=	£ 50,625	4
126,562									
379,688	×	0.25	=	£94,922	×	0.4	=	£ 37,969	5
94,922									
284,766									
200,000	=	Sale proceeds							
84,766	=	Balancing allowance	×		0.4	=	£ 33,906		6

26

Tax on trading profits/year

Sales	£1,400,000	
Materials	(300,000)	
Labour	(500,000)	
Taxed profit	600,000	Net trading cash flow
Tax at 40%	240,000	

Project cash flow (£000s)

Year	Machine cost	Machine tax relief	Trading c/f	Tax on trading	Working capital	Net project cash flow
0	(1200)				(150) =	(1350)
1		120	600		=	720
2		90	600	(240)	=	450
3		67.5	600	(240)	=	427.5
4		50.625	600	(240)	=	410.625
5	200	37.969	600	(240)	150 =	747.969
6		33.906		(240)	=	(206.094)

NPV Calculation

Year	Net cash flow	×	10% Discount factor	=	PV cash flow
0	(1,350,000)	×	1	=	(1,350,000)
1	720,000	×	0.9091	=	654,552
2	450,000	×	0.8264	=	371,880
3	427,500	×	0.7513	=	321,181
4	410,625	×	0.6830	=	280,457
5	747,969	×	0.6209	=	464,414
6	(206,094)	×	0.5645	=	(116,340)
			Net present value +		£ 626,144

Answer to problem 2

Contract 1: PV Costs (£000s)

	0	1	2
Special materials	30		
Other materials		100	110
Skilled labour		42	46.2
Unskilled labour		58.8	64.7
Total direct costs		200.8	220.9
Variable overheads (6% direct costs)		12.05	13.25
Total net cash flows	30	212.85	234.15
Discount factors	1	0.9091	0.9091 × 0.8621
	20	193.50	183.51

PV: £407.01

Contract 2: PV Costs (£000s)

	0	1	2
Other materials		120	132
Skilled labour		42	46.2
Unskilled labour		66.15	72.75
Direct costs		228.15	250.95
Variable overheads (6% direct costs)		13.7	15.05
Total net cash flows		241.85	266.0
Discount factors		0.9091	0.9091×0.8621
PV cash flows		219.87	208.47

PV: £428.34

NPV of Contract 1 produced in-house
+700,000 − 407,010 = +£292,990 NPV

NPV of Contract 2 produced in-house
+680,000 − 428,340 = +£251,660 NPV

NPV of Contract 1 when sub-contracted

PV cost: $245,000 + 245,000(1.10)^{-1}$ = − 467,730
Revenue = + 700,000
+£232,270 NPV

NPV of Contract 2 when sub-contracted

PV cost: $265,000 + 265,000(1.10)^{-1}$ = − 505,911
Revenue = + 680,000
+£174,089 NPV

The possible combinations open to Sparrow Ltd are:

Produce Contract 1	+ 292,990 NPV
Sub-contract Contract 2	+ 174,089 NPV
	+£467,079 Total NPV

Produce Contract 2	+ 251,660 NPV
Sub-contract Contract 1	+ 232,270 NPV
	+£483,930 Total NPV

Therefore the best option, given the constraints, is to produce Contract 2 in-house and sub-contract Contract 1. This results in the greatest amount of aggregate NPV.

Answer to problem 3

(a) *Net present value calculation in respect of the proposed production of Oakman*

Time period	*Workings*	t_1	t_2	t_3	t_4	t_5	t_6	t_7
Cash outflows								
Materials and other consumables	(1)		53,240	58,564	64,420	35,431	38,974	
Labour	(2)		45,626	52,470	60,341	34,696	39,900	
Redundancy payments	(3)				18,102			
Machine cost	(4)	229,900						
Machine overhaul	(5)			87,846				
Variable overheads	(6)		26,620	29,282	32,210	17,716	19,487	
Total outflows		229,900	125,486	228,162	175,073	87,843	98,361	
Cash inflows								
Redundancy payments saved	(7)	23,805						
Sales revenue	(8)		232,925	256,217	281,839	155,012	170,513	
Net cash flow before tax		(206,095)	107,439	28,055	106,766	67,169	72,152	25,460
WDA	(9)		(8,332)	20,116	15,087	11,315	8,486	(25,253)
Corporation tax at 35%				(37,604)	(9,819)	(37,368)	(23,509)	
After-tax cash flows		(206,095)	99,107	10,567	112,034	41,116	57,129	207
Present value factor at 20%		0.8333	0.6944	0.5787	0.4823	0.4019	0.3349	0.2791
Present value		(171,739)	68,820	6,115	54,034	16,524	19,133	58

Therefore, the project's NPV = –£7055

It is assumed that the NPV method of investment appraisal is suitable and acceptable to Bailey PLC. Based on the above NPV calculation, production of Oakman should not be undertaken because the project gives a negative NPV at 20% discount rate.

The NPV approach concentrates on the cashflow implications of the decision. Any item that does not have a cashflow consequence is being ignored. Therefore the information regarding depreciation is irrelevant. Head Office fixed costs are considered to be non-incremental, and do not change if Oakman is produced.

Workings

(1) *Materials and other consumables*

$$
\begin{aligned}
t_2 \quad & 5,000 \times £8 \times 1.10^3 = £53,240 \\
t_3 \quad & 5,000 \times £8 \times 1.10^4 = £58,564 \\
t_4 \quad & 5,000 \times £8 \times 1.10^5 = £64,420 \\
t_5 \quad & 2,500 \times £8 \times 1.10^6 = £35,431 \\
t_6 \quad & 2,500 \times £8 \times 1.10^7 = £38,974
\end{aligned}
$$

(2) *Labour*

$$
\begin{aligned}
t_2 \quad & 5,000 \times £3 \times 2 \times 1.15^3 = £45,626 \\
t_3 \quad & 5,000 \times £3 \times 2 \times 1.15^4 = £52,470 \\
t_4 \quad & 5,000 \times £3 \times 2 \times 1.15^5 = £60,341 \\
t_5 \quad & 2,500 \times £3 \times 2 \times 1.15^6 = £34,696 \\
t_6 \quad & 2,500 \times £3 \times 2 \times 1.15^7 = £39,900
\end{aligned}
$$

(3) *Redundancy payments*

$$
t_4 \quad 1,000 \text{ hrs} \times £3 \times 3 \times 1.15^5 = £18,102
$$

(4) *Machine cost*

$$
t_1 \quad £190,000 \times 1.10^2 = £229,900
$$

(5) *Machine overhaul*

$$
t_3 \quad £60,000 \times 1.10^4 = £87,846
$$

(6) *Variable overheads*

$$
\begin{aligned}
t_2 \quad & 5,000 \times £4 \times 1.10^3 = £26,620 \\
t_3 \quad & 5,000 \times £4 \times 1.10^4 = £29,282 \\
t_4 \quad & 5,000 \times £4 \times 1.10^5 = £32,210 \\
t_5 \quad & 2,500 \times £4 \times 1.10^6 = £17,716 \\
t_6 \quad & 2,500 \times £4 \times 1.10^7 = £19,487
\end{aligned}
$$

(7) *Redundancy payments saved*

This item represents the redundancy payments not required to be paid in one year's time to the six employees if Oakman is produced.

$$t_1 \quad 1{,}000 \text{ hrs} \times £3 \times 6 \times 1.15^2 = £23{,}805$$

(8) *Sales revenue*

$$
\begin{aligned}
t_2 \quad & 5{,}000 \times £35 \times 1.10^3 = £232{,}925 \\
t_3 \quad & 5{,}000 \times £35 \times 1.10^4 = £256{,}217 \\
t_4 \quad & 5{,}000 \times £35 \times 1.10^5 = £281{,}839 \\
t_5 \quad & 2{,}500 \times £35 \times 1.10^6 = £155{,}012 \\
t_6 \quad & 2{,}500 \times £35 \times 1.10^7 = £170{,}513
\end{aligned}
$$

(9) *Writing down allowance tax relief*

WDA		Tax relief	Year
$229{,}900 \times 0.25 = 57{,}475$	$\times 0.35 =$	$20{,}116$	3
$\underline{57{,}475}$			
$172{,}425 \times 0.25 = 43{,}106$	$\times 0.35 =$	$15{,}087$	4
$\underline{43{,}106}$			
$129{,}319 \times 0.25 = 32{,}330$	$\times 0.35 =$	$11{,}315$	5
$\underline{32{,}330}$			
$96{,}989 \times 0.25 = 24{,}247$	$\times 0.35 =$	$8{,}486$	6
$\underline{24{,}247}$			
$72{,}742 - 0 \quad = 72{,}742$	$\times 0.35 =$	$25{,}460$	7

(b) The existence of high rates of inflation principally cause additional forecasting problems as far as investment appraisal procedures are concerned. Hence the presence of inflation is a source of increased uncertainty in any investment appraisal. Two areas are affected: the forecast of the cash flow generated by the project, and the identification of the correct rate of discount. When using the NPV investment appraisal technique, the normal approach in evaluating a project within an inflationary environment is to forecast the expected money cash flows and then discount them to present value, using the money/market rate of discount.

It is probably the first of these two stages that causes the greatest problems. Any project consists of several individual cash-flow streams which arise from a number of different sources (e.g. sales revenues, labour wages, power costs) and they are likely to be affected by different rates of inflation, each of which requires to be forecasted. Furthermore, the effects of high rates of inflation on output prices and output quantities from a project create additional forecasting uncertainties, requiring knowledge of product elasticities and estimates of possible competitive and governmental actions.

The identification of the correct rate of discount causes fewer problems if the firm uses a capital market derived figure (e.g. the weighted average cost of capital or a CAPM required expected return), as capital market interest rates will include an allowance for anticipated general inflation.

In conclusion, therefore, the presence of high rates of inflation makes capital investment more risky, and investment appraisal more difficult.

7
Capital market imperfections

Answer to problem 1

(a) The conflict arises from the differing assumptions which the NPV and IRR methods make about the opportunity cost (or reinvestment rate) of generated cash flows. Given a perfect capital market, the NPV's assumption that their opportunity cost is equal to the market interest rate (for that level of risk) is correct. The IRR's assumption that their opportunity cost is equal to the IRR of the project which generates the cash flows is incorrect.

Therefore the company should accept the alternative with the largest positive NPV: the electrically powered vans. This selection will provide the greatest increase to shareholder wealth.

(b) Given that the situation is one of single-period capital rationing, the capital allocation problem can be solved using benefit–cost ratios:

Project	Benefit–cost ratio		Ranking
A	60/50	= 1.2	1
B	40/80	= 0.5	5
C	84/140	= 0.6	4
D	32/80	= 0.4	6
Petrol fleet (P-F)	80/100	= 0.8	2
Electrical fleet (E-F)	110.5/170	= 0.65	3

As projects P-F and E-F are mutually exclusive (the two van fleets) two alternative combinations of projects have to be evaluated, each containing one of the mutually exclusive alternatives:

Project	Outlay at t_0	
A	50	
P-F	100	NPV:
C	140	$60 + 80 + 84 = +£224,000$
	290	

33

Project	Outlay at t_0	
A	50	
E-F	170	NPV:
0.5C	70	$60 + 110.5 + 42 = £212,500$
	290	

Therefore, projects A, C and the petrol-powered van fleet should be accepted as this will provide the largest total of positive NPV, given the capital constraint.

(c) If the delivery fleet project were delayed by one year, their NPVs become:

P-F $£80/1.15 = £69,565$

E-F $£110.5/1.15 = £96,087$

Clearly, the electrically powered van fleet is the best alternative. Therefore, excluding the above from the capital rationing problem:

Project	Outlay at t_0	
A	50	
C	140	NPV:
B	80	$60 + 84 + 40 + 8 = £192,000$
$\frac{1}{4}$D	20	
	290	

Hence, the *total* NPV would be: $£192,000 + £96,087 = +£288,087$, which represents a gain of $£64,087$ over the original solution. This is the additional gain in shareholder wealth.

Answer to problem 2

(a) Accept all projects with NPV ≥ 0.

Project	NPV (£000s)	
A	+ 58.5	
B	+ 39.3	
C	− 20.7	Therefore, accept A, B, D and E.
D	+109.1	
E	+ 38.8	

(b) Using benefit–cost ratios: $\dfrac{\text{NPV}}{\text{rationed investment}}$

£000s

A	+58.5/100	=	0.585	3	
B	+39.3/50	=	0.786	2	
C	−20.7/100	=	−0.207	5	Ranking
D	+109.1/100	=	1.091	1	
E	+38.8/200	=	0.194	4	

£225,000 available, therefore accept D, B, 75% of A.

(c) The two alternative project combinations are:

	£000	£000
D, B, $37\frac{1}{2}$% of E	109.1 + 39.3 + 14.55 = 162.95 NPV	
D, A, $12\frac{1}{2}$% of E	109.1 + 58.5 + 4.85 = 172.45 NPV	

Therefore the best combination is D, A, and $12\frac{1}{2}$% of E.

(d) Examining all the different 'whole project' combinations shows that A and D produce the maximum amount of total NPV.

(e) Recalculating the benefit–cost ratios, now using t_1 outlays:

A	+58.5/100	=	0.585	3	
B	+39.3/100	=	0.393	4	
C	−20.7/–	=	–	–	Ranking
D	+109.1/50	=	2.182	1	
E	+38.8/50	=	0.776	2	

If project C is accepted, this makes an extra £100,000 of investment finance available at t_1; however, in doing so, a negative NPV (−£20,700) is incurred. Thus we will have to examine whether the extra +NPV generated by the additional investment finance outweighs this cost.

£150,000 of capital, accept D, E and 50% of A. Total NPV = £177,150.

£150,000 + £100,000 of capital, accept D, E, A, 50% of B *and* C. Total NPV = £205,350. This is the optimal combination.

(f) Let *a* equal the proportion of Project A undertaken,
     b   be the proportion of Project B undertaken,
     c   be the proportion of Project C undertaken,
     d   be the proportion of Project D undertaken, and
     e   be the proportion of Project E undertaken.

Objective Function

$$58.5a + 39.3b - 20.7c + 109.1d + 38.8e \qquad \text{MAX}$$

Constraints

$$100a + 50b + 200c + 100d + 200e \leq 225$$
$$100a + 100b + 50d + 50e \qquad \leq 150 + 100c$$
$$a, b, c, d, e \leq 1$$

Non-negativity conditions

$$a, b, c, d, e \geq 0$$

(g)

	DV of cash		+ 10% Discount factor	=	Total opportunity cost
Year 0	0.92	+	1.0	=	1.9200
Year 1	0.84	+	0.9091	=	1.7491
Year 2	0	+	0.8264	=	0.8264

The circumstances when a deposit account facility would be worthwhile would be when £1 × 1.9200 < £$(1 + i)$ × 1.7491

(h)

$$£1 \times 1.7491 = £1(1 + i) \times 0.8264$$

$$1.7491 = 0.8264 + 0.8264i$$

$$1.7491 - 0.8264 = 0.8264i$$

$$\frac{1.7491 - 0.8264}{0.8264} = i = 1.17 \text{ or } 117\% \text{ approximately.}$$

Therefore, the company would have to be offered a minimum rate of interest of 117% before they would be willing to transfer money from t_1 to t_2.

Answer to problem 3

(a) The investment strategy in single-period capital rationing is based on 'benefit–cost' ratios:

Project	NPV	÷	t_0 outlay	=	Benfit–cost ratios	Rank
A	+157.0	÷	400	=	+0.39	2
B	+150.0	÷	300	=	+0.50	1
C	+ 73.5	÷	300	=	+0.25	3
D	+159.5	÷	–	=	–	

Available cash	500
Invest:	300 in Project B
	200 Available
Invest:	200 in 50% Project A
	–

Project D will also be undertaken as it has a positive NPV and does not require cash in the rationed time period. Thus the complete investment plan is to undertake:

Project D, B and 50% of A

As a result, the total NPV generated will be:

$$159.5 + 150.0 + (0.50 \times 157.0) = \underline{+388 \text{ NPV}}$$

(b) Let *a* equal the proportion of Project A undertaken,
    b equal the proportion of Project B undertaken, and
    c equal the proportion of Project C undertaken.
Let *X* equal amount placed on deposit.

NPV of £1 placed on deposit

Year	Cash flow		10% discount		
0	-1	$\times$	1	$=$	-1
1	$+1.06$	$\times$	0.9091	$=$	$+0.96$
					$\overline{-0.04}$ NPV

LP formulation

Objective Function

$$157a + 150b + 73.5c + 159.5d - 0.04X \qquad \text{Max}$$

Constraints

$$
\begin{aligned}
400a + 300b + 300c + X &\leq 500 \\
200b + 300d &\leq 300 + 50a + 150c + 1.06X \\
a, b, c, d, &\leq 1
\end{aligned}
$$

Non-negativity Conditions

$$a, b, c, d, X \geq 0$$

(c) *Limitations of the formulation in part (b) above*
The linear programme can only be relied upon to produce an optimal solution to a capital rationing problem, if the assumptions inherent in its formulation hold. Therefore the investment allocation produced by the LP will only be optimal (i.e. will only maximize the objective function value) if:

(i) the information supplied and included in the formulation is certain and accurate;

(ii) all the relationships contained within the formulation are linear and divisible.

Under the first assumption, there are a number of points about which doubt is likely to exist.

(i)   Are all possible investment opportunities identified and included in the formulation?

(ii)   Are all the investment opportunities independent of each other, or are there some unspecified dependencies?

(iii)   Are the constraint levels accurate and fixed and have all possible constraints been included in the formulation? In particular, there may be unspecified resource constraints (other than finance), such as marketing constraints or maybe a constraint in terms of particular cash flow patterns that are unacceptable because of their implications for the company's published accounts.

Under the second assumption, points open to doubt include whether or not projects are truly divisible and, if they are divisible, whether the cost and revenue flows are linear (i.e. whether they exhibit constant returns to scale).

In addition, there are two special problems attached to the use of linear programming to solve the multi-period capital rationing problem.

(i)   The LP formulation assumes that all the project cash flows are certain and therefore it cannot effectively take account of the problem of uncertainty. The solution produced can only be considered optimal given this rather restrictive assumption.

(ii)   Two types of capital rationing can be specified: 'hard' and 'soft'. The essential distinction is the cause of the capital expenditure constraint. Where it is self-imposed by the company (e.g. when a capital budget is set internally) it can be termed soft capital rationing, whilst hard capital rationing is where the constraint is imposed externally by the capital markets. In this latter case, the LP solution to the capital rationing problem faces a dilemma over the identity of the correct period discount rate. When faced with an imperfect capital market, it should be represented by the return from the marginal investment in each rationed time period. However, this marginal investment cannot be identified until the capital rationing problem is solved and the problem cannot be solved until the rate of discount is known. Therefore, in circumstances of hard capital rationing, if an approximation of the correct period discount rate is used, the LP solution is likely to be only sub-optimal.

    In soft capital rationing circumstances, the correct discount rate is not a problem as long as it can be assumed that investors face a good/perfect capital market. This market rate of interest then represents their opportunity cost of capital and is therefore suitable to use as the rate of discount.

(d) *The existence of capital rationing in practice*

Capital rationing can be defined as a situation in which there are more apparently acceptable projects at the prevailing interest rate than can be financed. In considering the likelihood that a decision maker may be confronted by such a situation it is useful to distinguish the two types of rationing which may exist. Hard capital rationing is externally imposed. It is a situation in which the business is unable to raise any additional finance at any price. Soft capital rationing as was seen in part (c) is internally imposed.

It can be argued that hard capital rationing does not exist in the long run. If a firm has the investment opportunities and it looks hard enough it will be able to raise the requisite finance although it may need to pay a high price. Hard capital rationing is at worst a short-run market imperfection caused by lack of information and has no long-term significance.

An alternative view is that gaps in the institutional framework for providing finance may result in companies having no access to appropriate financial institutions and hence no access to investment funds at certain stages in their development. Therefore, it is at least possible that the market imperfections that give rise to hard capital rationing are more deep rooted and systematic than is implied in the question.

The remarks above are restricted to hard capital rationing. Soft rationing is a situation in which the limits on capital expenditure are imposed internally. It may seem irrational to refuse to accept projects whose return is in excess of the cost of capital. However, the motives for so doing are obvious. Many companies may exist where the owners are satisfied with the returns they are earning and have no wish to expand. It may be that while funds are available managerial expertise is limited and therefore it is necessary to restrict growth. Some firms may be reluctant to raise external funds, fearing some loss of control over the management of the business.

Irrational or not, there is little doubt that many firms do impose capital expenditure budgets internally. In these circumstances it is obviously necessary to have procedures for selecting between investment opportunities when there is a limit to the availability of capital.

8
Risk and expected return

Answer to problem 1

(a) The utility function can be derived by arbitrarily defining the utility of two levels of income and then using the relationships the investor has provided to calculate the utilities of the remaining levels of income.

Define $U(500) = 0$ and $U(4,500) = 1$. Then using the expected utility hypothesis it is possible to calculate the utility of £2,500 which must equal the expected utility of £500 with probability 0.4 and £4,500 with probability 0.6. Thus:

(i) $U(2,500) = 0.4 \ U(500) + 0.6 \ U(4,500)$
$U(2,500) = 0.4 \times 0 + 0.6 \times 1 = 0.6$

Similarly

(ii) $U(2,500) = 0.75 \ U(1,600) + 0.25 \ U(4,500)$
$0.6 = 0.75 \ U(1,600) + 0.25 \times 1$
$U(1,600) = 0.35/0.75 = 0.467$

(iii) $U(2,500) = 0.55 \ U(1,600) + 0.45 \ U(3,500)$
$0.6 = 0.55 \times 0.467 + 0.45 \ U(3,500)$
$U(3,500) = (0.6 - 0.55 \times 0.467)/0.45 = 0.763$

(iv) $U(2,500) = 0.75 \ U(2,000) + 0.25 \ U(3,500)$
$0.6 = 0.75 \ U(2,000) + 0.25 \times 0.763$
$U(2,000) = (0.6 - 0.25 \times 0.763)/0.75 = 0.546$

(v) $U(2,500) = 0.5 \ U(2,000) + 0.5 \ U(3,000)$
$0.6 = 0.5 \times 0.546 + 0.5 \ U(3,000)$
$U(3,000) = (0.6 - 0.5 \times 0.546)/0.5 = 0.654$

(vi) $U(2,500) = 0.85 \ U(2,000) + 0.15 \ U(4,000)$
$0.6 = 0.85 \times 0.546 + 0.15 \ U(4,000)$
$U(4,000) = (0.6 - 0.85 \times 0.546)/0.15 = 0.906$

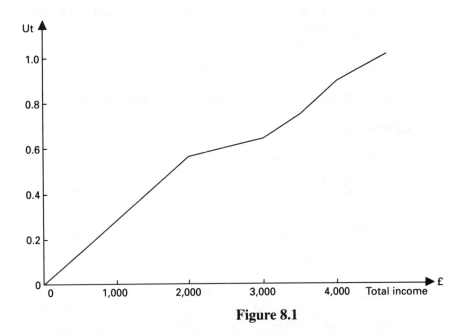

Figure 8.1

Therefore we have the following data:

$$
\begin{aligned}
U(500) &= 0 \\
U(1{,}600) &= 0.467 \\
U(2{,}000) &= 0.546 \\
U(2{,}500) &= 0.6 \\
U(3{,}000) &= 0.654 \\
U(3{,}500) &= 0.763 \\
U(4{,}000) &= 0.906 \\
U(4{,}500) &= 1.0
\end{aligned}
$$

Figure 8.1 illustrates this utility function. As can be seen from the graph, for a total income level of between (approximately) £0 and £2,500 the utility function is concave to the origin, indicating risk aversion. However, for income levels of between £2,500 and £4,000 the utility function is convex to the origin, suggesting that the investor becomes a risk seeker/risk lover.

(b) Note that the alternative activities are *additional*. As the utility function was drawn up using total income it can be used to compare the *total* incomes given by different alternatives.

Thus with (i) the total incomes will be £2,500 (1,500 + 1,000 already received), probability of 0.5, and £3,000 (2,000 + 1,000), probability of 0.5. The expected utility of (i) is thus:

$$
0.5 \; U(2{,}500) + 0.5 \; U(3{,}000) = 0.5 \; (0.6 + 0.654) = \underline{0.627}
$$

Similarly the total incomes from (ii) are 2,000 and 3,500 each with a probability of 0.5.

The expected utility of (ii) is thus:

$$0.5 \ U(2,000) + 0.5 \ U(3,500) = 0.5 \ (0.546 + 0.763) = \underline{0.655}$$

Thus (ii) is preferred by the investor as it has a higher utility.

(c) *Expected values*

(i)	(ii)
$2,500 \times 0.5 = \underline{1,250}$	$2,000 \times 0.5 = \underline{1,000}$
$3,000 \times 0.5 = \underline{1,500}$	$3,500 \times 0.5 = \underline{1,750}$
Expected value 2,750	2,750

Variances

(i)	(ii)
$(2,500 - 2,750)^2 \times 0.50 = \underline{31,250}$	$(2,000 - 2,750)^2 \times 0.5 = 281,250$
$(3,000 - 2,750)^2 \times 0.50 = \underline{31,250}$	$(3,500 - 2,750)^2 \times 0.5 = 281,250$
Variance $= \underline{62,500}$	Variance $= \underline{562,500}$

(d) (ii) is preferred by the investor even though it has a greater variance than (i) and the same expected value. Variance is a successful measure of risk where individuals are risk-averse. The investor is *not* risk-averse over the range of utilities of (i) and (ii).

9
Portfolio theory

Answer to problem 1

(a) In Fig. 9.1 AB, BC and AC are joined by straight lines since they are perfectly positively correlated.

   The shaded area represents possible risky portfolios. CML represents the capital market line. The market portfolio is risky Security B.

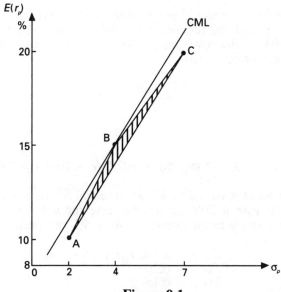

Figure 9.1

(b) The market price of risk is represented by the slope of CML:

$$\frac{0.15 - 0.08}{0.04} = \frac{0.07}{0.04} = 1.75$$

Therefore, investors will receive an expected return of 1.75% (in addition to the risk-free return) for every 1% increase in risk (standard deviation of return) that they accept, if they hold an efficient portfolio.

(c)   Investors would only be willing to hold risky Security B in possible combination with the risk-free security, assuming that all investors were risk-averse. This is because Security B gives the best 'price for risk', i.e. the maximum slope for the capital market line. Since A and C do not give as good a price for risk there must be a temporary disequilibrium; they are both giving a return which is too low for the risk involved.

(d)

$$E(r_p) = x \cdot E(r_M) + (1 - x)r_F$$
$$E(r_M) = 0.15$$
$$r_F \quad\ = 0.08$$
$$E(r_p) = 0.10$$
$$0.10 = 0.15x + (1 - x)\,0.08$$
$$0.10 = 0.15x + 0.08 - 0.08x$$
$$0.02 = 0.07x$$
$$\frac{0.02}{0.07} = x = 0.286$$

Thus the investor would place 28.6% of his investment capital in Security B and the remainder (71.4%) in the risk-free security.
    The risk of the resulting portfolio can either be calculated via the market price of risk:

$$\frac{0.10 - 0.08}{1.75} = 0.011$$

or via

$$\sigma_p = \sqrt{x^2} \cdot \sigma_M = \sqrt{(0.286^2 \times 0.04^2)} = 0.011$$

(e)   As the market portfolio yields an expected return of only 15% per period, to gain a 20% return, the investor will have to borrow additional funds at an interest cost of 8% per period:

$$E(r_p) = x \cdot E(r_M) + (1 - x)r_F$$
$$E(r_p) = 0.20$$
$$E(r_M) = 0.15$$
$$r_F \quad\ = 0.08 \text{ (borrowing cash)}$$
$$0.20 = 0.15x + (1 - x)\,0.08$$
$$0.20 = 0.15x + 0.08 - 0.08x$$
$$0.12 = 0.07x$$
$$\frac{0.12}{0.07} = x = 1.714$$

Therefore an investor will borrow an amount equivalent to 71.4% of his own funds. These borrowings, together with his own investment funds, will be placed in Security B.

The risk attached to this portfolio yielding a 20% expected period return is as follows: via the market price of risk

$$\sigma_p = \frac{0.20 - 0.08}{1.75}$$

$$= 0.0686$$

or

$$\sigma_p = \sqrt{x^2 \cdot \sigma_M^2} = \sqrt{(1.714^2 \times 0.04^2)}$$

$$= 0.0686$$

(f) (i) Information about the characteristics of the securities is freely available.
(ii) There are no transaction costs.
(iii) Investors are rational and risk-averse.
(iv) Investors measure risk by the standard deviation of the expected returns.
(v) All investors face the same investment opportunities, have the same expectations about the future and make decisions with a time horizon of one time period ahead.

From the construction of the capital market line can be developed the capital asset pricing model (CAPM), which gives the required return from an inefficient investment (e.g. a project undertaken by a firm) when the company's shares will be held as part of an efficient portfolio. This pricing model shows that a project's minimum acceptable return does not depend upon its total risk, but just on that part of its risk which cannot be eliminated through holding it as part of an efficient portfolio, i.e. systematic risk. Unsystematic risk is effectively diversified away if the project is held by investors as part of an efficient investment portfolio.

However the CAPM represents a single-period return and so it must be used with care in a multi-period NPV analysis.

Answer to problem 2

(a) *Hong Kong*

HK$m		HK$/£		£m	Outlay		£NPV		Prob.	
63.8	÷	12.7625	=	4.9990	− 5.2	=	−0.201	×	0.30 =	−0.0603
64.4	÷	12.7625	=	5.0460	− 5.2	=	−0.154	×	0.40 =	−0.0616
64.9	÷	12.7625	=	5.0852	− 5.2	=	−0.1148	×	0.30 =	−0.0344
							E(NPV)		=	−£0.1563

$(£NPV)^2 \times Prob.$

$$
\begin{array}{ll}
0.0404 \quad \times 0.30 = 0.0121 & \\
0.0237 \quad \times 0.40 = 0.0095 & \text{Risk} = \sqrt{0.0256} - (-0.1563)^2 = £0.03\text{m} \\
0.0132 \quad \times 0.30 = \underline{0.0040} & \\
\quad E(NPV)^2 \quad = \overline{0.0256} &
\end{array}
$$

Switzerland

SFFm	SFF/£	£m	Outlay	£NPV	Prob.	
15.39	÷ 2.4400	= 6.3074	−5.2	= +1.1074 ×	0.35 =	0.3876
15.80	÷ 2.4400	= 6.4754	−5.2	= +1.2754 ×	0.40 =	0.5102
16.34	÷ 2.4400	= 6.6967	−5.2	= +1.4967 ×	0.25 =	0.3742
					E(NPV) =	£+1.2720

$(£NPV)^2 \times Prob.$

$$
\begin{array}{ll}
1.2263 \quad \times 0.35 = 0.4292 & \\
1.6266 \quad \times 0.40 = 0.6506 & \text{Risk} = \sqrt{1.7298} - (1.2720)^2 = £0.33\text{m} \\
2.2401 \quad \times 0.25 = \underline{0.5600} & \\
\quad E(NPV)^2 \quad = \overline{1.7298} &
\end{array}
$$

Greece

DRm	DR/£	£m	Outlay	£NPV	Prob.	
1620	÷ 225.7250	= 7.1769	−5.2	= +1.9769 ×	0.30 =	0.5931
1700	÷ 225.7250	= 7.5313	−5.2	= +2.3313 ×	0.50 =	1.1656
1730	÷ 225.7250	= 7.6642	−5.2	= +2.4642 ×	0.20 =	0.4928
					E(NPV) =	£+2.2515m

$(£NPV)^2 \times Prob.$

$$
\begin{array}{ll}
3.9081 \quad \times 0.30 = 1.1724 & \\
5.4350 \quad \times 0.50 = 2.7175 & \text{Risk} = \sqrt{5.1044} - (2.2515)^2 = £0.19\text{m} \\
6.0723 \quad \times 0.20 = \underline{1.2145} & \\
\quad E(NPV)^2 \quad = \overline{5.1044} &
\end{array}
$$

Singapore

S$m	S$/£	£m	Outlay	£NPV	Prob.	
18.1	÷ 3.4422	= 5.2583	−5.2	= 0.0583 ×	0.30 =	0.0175
19.3	÷ 3.4422	= 5.6069	−5.2	= 0.4069 ×	0.40 =	0.1628
25.9	÷ 3.4422	= 7.5243	−5.2	= 2.3243 ×	0.30 =	0.6973
					E(NPV) =	£+0.8776m

$(£NPV)^2 \times Prob.$

$$
\begin{array}{ll}
0.0034 \quad \times 0.30 = 0.0010 & \\
0.1656 \quad \times 0.40 = 0.0662 & \text{Risk} = \sqrt{1.6879} - (0.8776)^2 = £0.96\text{m} \\
5.4024 \quad \times 0.30 = \underline{1.6207} & \\
\quad E(NPV)^2 \quad = \overline{1.6879} &
\end{array}
$$

Summary

	Hong Kong	Switzerland	Greece	Singapore	Austria
E(NPV) (£m)	(0.1563)	1.2720	2.2515	0.8776	(0.11)
Standard deviation:					
Risk (£m)	0.03	0.33	0.19	0.96	0.80

On the face of it, the Hong Kong and Austrian opportunities should be rejected as they produce negative NPVs. Therefore, the choice is between Switzerland, Greece and Singapore. Given the restriction imposed by Alpha, there are just two options:

Switzerland and Singapore
Greece and Singapore

although a third opportunity – Hong Kong and Switzerland – might be worth investigating, despite the Hong Kong project's negative NPV, because of the negative correlation coefficient between the two countries.

The E(NPV) of the three portfolios would be:

Switzerland/Singapore : + £1,2720m + £0.8776m = +£2.1496
Greece/Singapore : + £2.2515m + £0.8776m = +£3.1291
Switzerland/Hong Kong : + £1.2720m − £0.1563m = +£1.1157

and, using the equation for the risk of a two-asset portfolio, where the weights, (x and $[1 - x]$) are 0.5 and 0.5, respectively, as all projects require the same outlay, the risk of the three possible portfolios would be:

Switzerland/Singapore : £0.55m
Greece/Singapore : £0.54m
Switzerland/Hong Kong : £0.16m

From this it can be seen that the Greece and Singapore combination dominates the Switzerland and Singapore combination; it has a higher expected NPV and a lower level of risk. Thus the company is likely to select the Greece and Singapore combination. However, if the company was highly risk-averse, it *may* decide to go for the Switzerland and Hong Kong combination because of its much lower level of risk (and despite its much lower expected NPV).

(b) (i) The main criticism of the approach used to evaluate the investment alternatives arises from the fact that they have been considered in isolation from Alpha PLC's existing activities. Such an approach might be justified only if it could be assumed that Europe and the Far East were completely segmented markets and had a zero correlation coefficient with Alpha's existing UK activities. Such an assumption would be highly unrealistic.

Therefore the risk levels calculated for the three alternative investment combinations simply indicate their total combined risk. They do not indicate what impact their acceptance would have on Alpha's existing level of *total* risk, nor do they indicate what impact the investment opportunities would have on Alpha's existing level of *systematic* risk (i.e. Alpha's beta value).

The analysis is therefore inadequate from the viewpoint of Alpha's management, who *personally* may be interested in the investment's impact on the company's *total* risk (because they hold undiversified 'work' portfolios), and it is also inadequate from the viewpoint of Alpha's shareholders. Shareholders can be assumed to have well-diversified investment portfolios and therefore will be interested, not in the total risk of the investment opportunities, but purely in their systematic risk and the effect that they will have on Alpha's beta value.

(ii) The expected net present values considered can also be criticized on the grounds of the discount rate used and the exchange rates used. (Chapter 18 covers this area in detail.)

The calculation of an overseas project's NPV can be undertaken in either of two ways. One is to convert the overseas currency cash flows to domestic currency cash flows and then discount at the domestic discount rate which reflects the project's systematic risk. The alternative is to discount the overseas currency cash flows to present value using the appropriate overseas discount rate and then to convert the resulting NPV to a domestic currency NPV at the spot rate.

In this case, the company has apparently chosen the latter course of action, discounting the overseas cash flows to present value. However, they have used the same discount rate (20%) in all cases. This is incorrect on two counts. One is that the discount rate should reflect the systematic risk of the project under evaluation and it is unlikely that all five projects have the same degree of systematic risk. The other is that the discount rate used should have varied from country to country to take account of differences in interest and inflation rates.

Finally, the analysis can be criticized on the grounds that the exchange rates used were estimates of the *average* rates over the next five years. Except in the case where a project's cash flows arise *evenly* over its life, such an approach would be incorrect and estimates of year-by-year exchange rates should be used. However, given the approach taken to calculating the E(NPVs) on these projects (see above), it is the current *spot* rates which should have been used, not the average future exchange rates.

Answer to problem 3

(i)
$$E[r_p] = x \cdot E[r_A] + (1 - x) \cdot E[r_B]$$
$$E[r_p] = (0.8 \times 12) + (0.2 \times 20) = 13.6\%$$

(ii) $\sigma_p = \sqrt{x^2 \sigma_A^2 + (1 - x)^2 \sigma_B^2 + 2x(1 - x)\sigma_A \sigma_B \rho_{AB}}$

$\sigma_p = \sqrt{(0.8^2 \times 3^2) + (0.2^2 \times 7^2) + (2 \times 0.8 \times 0.2 \times 3 \times 7 \times 0.1)}$

$\sigma_p = \underline{2.9\%}$

(iii) The weighted average risk of the portfolio is:

$$(0.8 \times 3\%) + (0.2 \times 7\%) = 3.8\%$$

The actual risk of the portfolio, as calculated in part (ii) above is 2.9%. Thus a significant amount of risk reduction has been achieved through portfolio diversification. The reason for such a significant degree of risk reduction (0.9% as a percentage of 3.8% represents 23.7% risk reduction) is that the correlation coefficient, at a value of +0.1, is well away from +1.

(iv) It is possible to construct a zero-risk two-asset portfolio, if the correlation coefficient is perfectly negative: −1.
  In such circumstances, the equation for portfolio risk reduces to:

$$\sigma_p = x\sigma_A - (1 - x)\sigma_B$$

Therefore, solving for x:

$$0 = x \cdot 3\% - (1 - x)\ 7\%$$
$$0 = 3\%x - 7\% + 7\%x$$
$$7\% = 10\%x$$
$$\frac{7\%}{10\%} = x = 0.70$$

Therefore 70% of the funds should be placed in Project A and the other 30% in Project B.

10
The capital asset pricing model

Answer to problem 1

(a) As $\beta_{co} = \dfrac{\text{Systematic risk of Co.}}{\text{Risk of market portfolio}}$

then Systematic Risk of Co = Risk Market Portfolio $\times \beta_{co}$

and, given:

$$\beta_{x+y} = \left[\beta_x \cdot \frac{x}{x+y}\right] + \left[\beta_y \cdot \frac{y}{x+y}\right]$$

then

$$\beta_{V+A} = \left[0.67 \times \frac{62}{66}\right] + \left[0.67 \times \frac{4}{66}\right] \quad = 0.67 \times 16\% = \underline{10.72\%}$$
$$\text{(i)}$$

$$\beta_{V+B} = \left[0.67 \times \frac{62}{66}\right] + \left[1.14 \times \frac{4}{66}\right] \quad = 0.698 \times 16\% = \underline{11.17\%}$$
$$\text{(ii)}$$

$$\beta_{V+C} = \left[0.67 \times \frac{62}{66}\right] + \left[0.88 \times \frac{4}{66}\right] \quad = 0.683 \times 16\% = \underline{10.93\%}$$
$$\text{(iii)}$$

In all three cases, the new market value of the company would be expected to be: £62m + £4m = £66 million.

(b) Portfolio theory shows that when assets are combined, the total risk of the combination (measured as standard deviation of returns) is less than a weighted average of the risks of the individual assets, as long as the assets are less than perfectly positively correlated with each other. The further away the correlation coefficient is from being perfectly positive (i.e. +1), the greater will be the amount of risk reduction.

The simplest type of portfolio is a two-asset portfolio. Vanhal, plus an acquired company, could be viewed as such a portfolio. For example, if Vanhal were to acquire company A, then the total risk of the enlarged company would be given by:

$$\sigma_{V+A} = \sqrt{x^2\sigma_V^2 + (1 - x)^2 \sigma_A^2 + 2x(1 - x)\sigma_V\sigma_A\rho_{V,A}}$$

where x and $(1 - x)$ represent the proportions of Vanhal and A represented in the enlarged company. As long as the correlation coefficient $(\rho_{V,A})$ is less than $+1$, then σ_{V+A} will be less than $(\sigma_V \cdot x) + \sigma_A \cdot (1 - x)$. In other words, Vanhal will have been able to reduce its total risk (in the sense that the resulting total risk will be less than a weighted average of the total risk of the components) through the diversification process.

(c) There could be a large number of possible reasons why the directors of Vanhal might wish to diversify, but the question indicates that the primary reason is to broaden the company's activities. In this respect, the desire of the directors to diversify arises from their wish to reduce the total risk of the company. How this may be done – in relation to the company's stock exchange return – has been shown in the answer to part (b). However, from the directors' viewpoint, risk reduction through diversification would manifest itself in a reduction in the variability of the company's operating cash flow and therefore resulting (in stock market parlance) in an increase in the perceived 'quality' of the company's earnings.

The directors would be interested in trying to bring about such an effect for two reasons. One would be to hope for an enhancement of the stock market price of the company's shares through the increased earnings quality leading to a higher Price-Earnings ratio multiple being applied to the company's earnings per share. However, such an effect would only come about if the market valued total risk, rather than just systematic risk.

The second reason for the directors' interest in such a policy would be the benefits that a more stable corporate cash flow would bring to the job of management. For example, there would be a reduced probability of insolvency (and the consequential costs for directors); there may be opportunities for increasing the company's gearing; a stable dividend policy might be able to be maintained with greater ease; and generally the task of managing the overall company would become less demanding.

To suggest which of the three companies under consideration best meet the directors' requirements is difficult, given the information available. As all three are in the same area of industry, any one of the three would presumably provide the required broadening of the company's activities. However, assuming that the directors are interested in such a move in order to reduce total corporate risk, then they may not be indifferent between the three companies. Given that all three companies have the same value, and assuming that they all have the same correlation coefficient with Vanhal (which is not unrealistic, given the circumstances), then company A is likely to be preferable as it has the smallest amount of total risk and specific risk. (Non-specific or systematic risk cannot be diversified away.) If the assumption about the correlation coefficient is unsafe, then the company best suiting the directors' requirements would be that whose combination of total risk and correlation coefficient – used in the expression given in answer to part (b) above – would result in the lowest level of total risk for the enlarged company.

(d) Portfolio theory and the capital asset pricing model suggest that investors should only be interested in systematic risk. As systematic risk cannot be diversified away, there would be no risk reduction benefits accruing to shareholders as a result of the merger, assuming that they already hold well-diversified investment portfolios.

In fact such a move as that contemplated by Vanhal may be unwelcome to shareholders if it were to significantly change the total market value and beta of the company. In such circumstances, a shareholder holding a diversified portfolio with a desired beta value would have to adjust his/her portfolio (and so incur transaction costs) in the light of the change to Vanhal.

Despite the foregoing, shareholders might still welcome the take-over, even given the assumption in part (a) of the question that there are no synergy benefits. For example, shareholders holding non-fully-diversified portfolios would gain some risk reduction effect. Alternatively, if the company taken over was worth more than the £4m purchase price, then Vanhal's shareholders' wealth would increase. Again if, as a result of the take-over, Vanhal were able to increase their debt capacity, then the tax shield benefits (if they exist) would also accrue to the shareholders (see Chapter 15).

However, given a reasonably efficient capital market with shareholders holding well-diversified investment portfolios, the value to shareholders of such a take-over as that proposed is likely to be minimal. In fact, the costs (both internally and externally to Vanhal) associated with the take-over may result in shareholders suffering an actual reduction in their wealth.

Answer to problem 2

(a) Given that Mr Swift has a well-diversified portfolio, it will be safe to assume that most of the unsystematic risk that is attached to the individual securities in the portfolio will have been diversified away. Thus his portfolio risk will largely consist of systematic risk and so the variance of returns on his portfolio will essentially measure systematic risk.

If he wishes to include shares that will reduce his portfolio variance, then he will be concerned with the covariance of returns between any new share and his existing portfolio. In other words, he is interested in selecting the shares of that company which would help to bring the greatest reduction in portfolio risk. This would be indicated by looking at the product of the standard deviation of returns and the correlation with Mr Swift's existing portfolio:

$$\text{Dove: } \sigma_D \times \rho_{D,S} = 35\% \times 0.16 = 5.6\%$$

$$\text{Jay: } \quad \sigma_J \times \rho_{J,S} = 30\% \times 0.21 = 6.3\%$$

Under these circumstances, the optimal course of action for Mr Swift – given his objective – would be to invest in the shares of Dove plc.

(b) The CAPM shows that there is a positive relationship between the expected return on a security and its degree of systematic risk – which is normally measured by its beta value. Thus, the greater the amount of systematic risk the greater will be the expected return demanded by investors in an equilibrium stock market. The systematic risk of individual securities can be measured as the product of their standard deviation of return and their correlation coefficient with the market portfolio. In the case of Dove and Jay, this gives values for systematic risk of:

$$\text{Dove: } \sigma_D \times \rho_{D,M} = 35\% \times 0.3 \ = 10.5\%$$

$$\text{Jay: } \quad \sigma_J \times \rho_{J,M} = 30\% \times 0.25 = \ 7.5\%$$

As Dove plc has the higher level of systematic risk, it would follow that Dove should have the higher expected return, as indeed it does: 9% as against only 7% for Jay plc.

(c) If Mr Swift's portfolio contained shares in a few companies only, then he would be holding a largely undiversified portfolio. Hence, the variance of returns of the portfolio would reflect both the systematic and unsystematic risk components as there would be insufficient diversification to wash out the unsystematic risk.

Without passing comment on whether such a portfolio is wise (although it would appear sensible for Mr Swift to diversify further), in order to meet his objective on portfolio variance Mr Swift would be most interested in selecting that company which would help to bring the greatest reduction to the total risk of his existing portfolio.

However, in these particular circumstances a problem arises from the fact that with small portfolios a security's contribution to portfolio risk can arise out of its own variance, as well as from its covariance with the existing portfolio. Thus, although Dove plc, as was seen in the answer to (a), has the smaller covariance with the existing portfolio, it has a higher variance (or standard deviation) than Jay:

$$\sigma_D^2 = 0.1225 \qquad \sigma_J^2 = 0.09$$

Therefore the final choice between the two companies will depend upon the existing components of Mr Swift's portfolio and their weights and the resulting changes brought about through the introduction of the new security.

(d) Shareholders, assuming that they hold well-diversified efficient portfolios, will be interested in the effect on the risk of their portfolio of the addition to it of any particular security. However, because the portfolio is fully diversified, when a new share is added (again, assuming that only a marginal investment is made), then that new share's unsystematic risk is eliminated, or is washed out, and it is only the systematic risk that is added to the portfolio. It is therefore for this reason that the relevant measure of risk for a company's shareholders is the amount of systematic risk. This is most conveniently measured in relative terms via the beta value.

Debt holders are also interested in the systematic risk of their investment which, again, could be measured by beta. However, as most debt is unquoted, beta does not provide a convenient measure of risk. Hence debt holders attempt to measure the risk of a company's debt through a series of alternative measures including the degree of capital gearing, the interest cover ratio, the amount of tangible assets held by the company and the stability, or otherwise, of the company's annual net cash flow. Just which of these factors contribute to systematic risk and which to unsystematic risk is somewhat unclear. What evidence there is available suggests that all four factors – with the possible exception of the amount of tangible assets held – are likely to contribute to systematic risk.

Finally, managers, as far as their labour is concerned, hold undiversified portfolios. Therefore, unlike outside investors, they are interested in the total risk of a company and – in particular – the likelihood that it will fall. Thus, managers are likely to measure risk by the variability of net annual cash flows (i.e. by the variance of corporate net cash flows), the skew of those cash flows and by the degree of capital gearing. All three factors will have a bearing on the riskiness of the company as seen from management's viewpoint.

Answer to problem 3

(a) (i) *Expected return on Cemenco equity*
Average % annual capital gain

$$[16.42 \div 9.50]^{1/3} - 1 = \underline{20\%}$$

Average % dividend yield

$$[10\% + 12\% + 8\% + 10\%] \div 4 = \underline{10\%}$$

Therefore, expected return on Cemenco shares = 20% + 10% = $\underline{30\%}$

(ii) *Expected return on TSE Index*
Average % annual capital gain

$$[1983 \div 1490]^{1/3} - 1 = \underline{10\%}$$

Average % dividend yield

$$[16\% + 15\% + 10\% + 18\%] \div 4 = \underline{15\%}$$

Therefore, expected return on the TSE Index = 10% + 15% = $\underline{25\%}$

(iii) *Return on Government stocks*

$$15\% + 16\% + 14\% + 15\% \div 4 = \underline{15\%}$$

Therefore, risk free return = $r_f = \underline{\underline{15\%}}$

(iv) *Beta value of Cemenco equity*

$$E[r_c] = r_f + (E[r_m] - r_f) \cdot \beta_c$$

Therefore:

$$\frac{E[r_c] - r_f}{E[r_m] - r_f} = \beta_c = \frac{30\% - 15\%}{25\% - 15\%} = \frac{15}{10} = \underline{\underline{1.50}}$$

(b) It is difficult to predict with any accuracy whether the Government's action will make Cemenco Ltd more or less systematically risky. Although in total risk terms the risk of the company will be reduced, it is difficult to be certain what will be the effect on systematic risk. The company's revenues will, as always, be fairly sensitive to the level of Trinka's economic activity and this is unlikely to change by being given a monopoly. However, there will be price control and this may therefore result in increasing the company's systematic risk exposure.

Answer to problem 4

(a) The beta value of Mr Smith's savings portfolio is simply a weighted average of the individual portfolio elements. Given that Treasury Stock has a beta value of zero, then the portfolio beta is:

$$(0.20 \times 0.10) + (0.80 \times 0.10) + (1.20 \times 0.10) + (1.6 \times 0.20)$$
$$+ (0 \times 0.50) = \underline{0.54}$$

In order to calculate the expected return on the savings portfolio, it is first necessary to estimate the average market risk premium. Using the CAPM expression and the Company W shares, this can be found as follows:

$$E[r_W] = r_F + (E[r_M] - r_F) \cdot \beta_W$$
$$7.6\% = 6\% + (E[r_M] - r_F) \cdot 0.20$$
$$\frac{7.6\% - 6\%}{0.20} = (E[r_M] - r_F) = \underline{8\%}$$

Thus the expected return on Mr Smith's savings portfolio will be:

$$E[r_p] = 6\% + (8\%) \times 0.54 = 10.32\%$$

(b) If Mr Smith wants a savings portfolio with an expected return of 12%, then his portfolio beta will need to be:

$$12\% = 6\% + (8\%) \times \beta_p$$
$$\frac{12\% - 6\%}{(8\%)} = \beta_p = \underline{0.75}$$

His existing shareholding is going to remain unchanged and so that will contribute a β of 0.54 to the beta of his savings portfolio. Therefore he will want to invest a sufficient proportion of his savings in the market portfolio (which, by definition, has a $\beta_m = 1$) to bring his overall portfolio β up to 0.75.
   Let x = proportion of his savings placed in the market portfolio:

$$0.75 = (x \cdot 1) + 0.54$$
$$\frac{0.75 - 0.54}{1} = x = 0.21$$

Thus Mr Smith should place 21% of his savings in the market portfolio. This represents an amount of: $0.21 \times £12,000 = £2,520$. Thus he should sell £2,520 of Treasury Bills and invest the money in the market portfolio.
   His total, revised portfolio would now be:

Investment	Worth
Treasury Bills	£3,480
Market portfolio	£2,520
Company W shares	£1,200
Company X shares	£1,200
Company Y shares	£1,200
Company Z shares	£2,400

(c) To construct an efficient portfolio yielding an expected return of 10.32% would require (as we know from the answer to (a)) a portfolio β of 0.54.

Given that $\beta_M = 1$ and $\beta_F = 0$, this efficient portfolio β could be constructed by placing 54% of the saving into the market portfolio and the remainder in Treasury Bills:

£6,480 invested in market portfolio
£5,520 invested in Treasury Bills

(d) Both Mr Smith's original portfolio, and the one given in the answer to part (c), give an expected return of 10.32%. However, it would be better for Mr Smith to choose the part (c) portfolio.

The reason for this advice is that this latter portfolio represents an *efficient* portfolio which lies along the capital market line. As such Mr Smith would be holding the very least possible amount of risk for his expected return of 10.32%. In particular, he would have eliminated all unsystematic risk.

In contrast, his existing portfolio is inefficient in that although it contains the same amount of systematic risk as the efficient portfolio constructed in (c), it will also contain *unsystematic* risk. This is because Mr Smith's existing portfolio is relatively undiversified and much of the unsystematic risk remains. Thus although the two portfolios produce the same expected return, Mr Smith's existing portfolio is far riskier (in terms of systematic and unsystematic risk) than the efficient portfolio suggested in the answer to part (c).

(e) In theory neither alpha nor beta values should be of significance to investors. All that investors need ensure is that they invest in the market portfolio (and Treasury Bills), and that they locate their own personal portfolio in whatever is the desired point on the capital market line. However, in practice, investors are often interested in both alpha and beta values of shares.

A share's beta value indicates its level of systematic risk relative to the average level of systematic risk on the stock market. Thus investors who wish to hold a portfolio of shares with (say) a high overall beta will wish to identify those companies whose shares have high beta values, in order to include them in their portfolio.

In practice, beta values of shares are estimated by regressing the monthly historical returns on an individual company's shares against the return on a surrogate of the market portfolio: the return on the stock market index. This regression line is known as the characteristic line, and its slope provides the estimate of beta.

The point where the regression line/characteristic line cuts the vertical axis is referred to as the alpha value of the share. Alpha values can be either positive or negative (or zero), depending upon whether the regression line cuts the vertical axis above or below the origin of the axes. In theory, the regression line should pass through the origin, but in practice it usually does not do so because of the presence of unsystematic risk.

Thus a share whose characteristic line has a *positive* alpha value has produced a return *above* the expected return over the regression period. This above-average return (termed a positive abnormal return) is caused by the presence of unsystematic risk. In theory, over time, this unsystematic risk – and hence the positive abnormal return – should be eliminated through the diversification effect. On this reasoning, some investors like to invest in shares with *negative* alpha values – that is, invest in shares which have produced below their expected return – on the basis that this will be counteracted with an off-setting above expected return in the future. If such an investment strategy were to work it would, of course, represent a market inefficiency.

11

Traditional approaches to risk

Answer to problem 1

(a) The first task with this type of complex ENPV question is to identify the different 'states of the world' and their associated probabilities. Once this is done, the project's NPV in each state of the world can be calculated. These state of the world NPVs are then each multiplied by their associated probabilities and added together to give the overall *expected* NPV or ENPV of the project.

The states of the world
There are three stages involved with this project.

Stage 1   The seismic survey. There is a 50% chance that this will reveal that the geology indicates the possibility of oil. If it does, we proceed to the next stage. But there is also a 50% chance (i.e. $1.0 - 0.50 = 0.50$) that the geology indicates that there will be no oil. Under these circumstances, the company goes no further and abandons the project.

Stage 2   The exploration wells. If the seismic survey indicates the possibility of oil then the company will proceed to drill exploration wells to see if oil does actually occur. There is a 30% chance that the exploration well will discover oil, in which case we proceed to stage 3. However, there is a 70% chance (i.e. $1.0 - 0.30 = 0.70$) that the exploration well will indicate *no* oil is present. Under the circumstances, the company will go no further and abandon the project.

Stage 3   The appraisal wells. If the exploration wells indicate oil then we will proceed to drill appraisal wells to identify just what quantity of oil is there. There is a 60% chance that the oil will be in negligible quantities (what the question refers to as type I). In those circumstances, the project is then obviously abandoned. However, there is a 32% chance that the appraisal wells will indicate the presence of 42m barrels of oil (type II) and an 8% chance that 2,250m barrels of oil will be indicated (type III). Under each of these last two circumstances the company will then proceed to extract the oil.

As a result, there are five possible outcome combinations, or states of the world.

State A Seismic survey indicates no oil and the project is abandoned.

State B Seismic survey indicates that there may be oil, an exploration well is drilled and finds no oil. The project is then abandoned.

State C Seismic survey indicates that there may be oil, an exploration well is drilled and also indicates oil. Therefore an appraisal well is drilled, but a negligible amount of oil is found. The project is abandoned.

State D This is the same as for State C, except the appraisal well discovers 42 million barrels of oil which the company then extracts.

State E Again, the same as for State C, except the appraisal well discovers 2,250 million barrels of oil which the company then extracts.

The probability of occurence of each of these five states can be found from the product of the probability of each event in each state.

State A   0.50 or 50%
State B   0.50 × 0.70 = 0.35 or 35%
State C   0.50 × 0.30 × 0.60 = 0.09 or 9%
State D   0.50 × 0.30 × 0.32 = 0.048 or 4.8%
State E   0.50 × 0.30 × 0.08 = 0.012 or 1.2%

The required information
Having identified the separate states of the world and their associated probabilities, the next stage is to work out the project's NPV under each state. However, before doing that, we need to assemble the required information.

(i)   The first item of information is to identify the annual oil production pattern in the two states (D and E) where oil is actually produced. From the information in the question, the following can be derived.

> *State D* 14m barrels per year output for the first two years of the oilfield's life and 7m barrels per year for the second two years: 14m + 14m + 7m + 7m = 42m
>
> *State E* 300m barrels per year output for the first five years of the oilfield's life and then 150m barrels per year for each of the remaining five years: (5 × 300m) + (5 × 150m) = 2,250m.

(ii) As all the other financial figures are provided in £ terms, we need to express the oil revenues similarly. At $26.40 a barrel and an exchange rate of $1.20 = £1, the £ revenue from a barrel is $26.40 ÷ 1.20 = £22.

(iii) The operating net cash flow (pre-tax) per barrel is: £22 × 0.45 = £9.90.

(iv) The annual revenues (pre-tax) will be:

$$7m \text{ barrels} = £69.3m$$
$$14m \text{ barrels} = £138.6m$$
$$140m \text{ barrels} = £1,485m$$
$$300m \text{ barrels} = £2,970m$$

(v) The annual tax cash flow on these net revenues are as follows:

$$£69.3m × 0.77 = £53.361m$$
$$£138.6m × 0.77 = £106.722m$$
$$£1485.0m × 0.77 = £1143.45m$$
$$£2970.0m × 0.77 = £2286.9m$$

(vi) Finally, there is the *timing* of cash flows and the discount rate. The licence fee of £20m and the seismic survey cost of £2m both occur at Year 0. The appraisal wells cost of £100m and the exploration well cost of £10m both occur at Year 1. All exploration costs receive tax relief at 50%. The first oil production revenues occur at Year 2 and the first tax charge occurs at Year 3. The discount rate is 16%.

The NPV Calculations (£ millions)
In these calculations (which really test your discounting ability), use can be made of the fact that a lot of the cash flows are annuities.

State A	Year 0	−20		−2			= −22		= −22.00
	Year 1		+10		+1		= $+11(1.16)^{-1}$		= + 9.48
								NPV	= −12.52

State B	Year 0	−20		−2			= −22		= −22.00
	Year 1		+10		+1	−10	= $+1(1.16)^{-1}$		= + 0.86
	Year 2					+5	= $+5(1.16)^{-2}$		= + 3.72
								NPV	= −17.42

State C Year 0 −20   −2   = −22
         Year 1   +10   +1 −10   −100   = −99
         Year 2   +5   +50   = +55

Year 0 −22   = −22.00
Year 1 −99(1.16)$^{-1}$ = −85.35
Year 2 +55(1.16)$^{-2}$ = +40.88

$$\text{NPV} = -66.47$$

State D −22 −99(1.16)$^{-1}$ +55(1.16)$^{-2}$ +138.6A$_{\overline{2}|0.16}$ (1.16)$^{-1}$
−106.722 A$_{\overline{2}|0.16}$ (1.16)$^{-2}$ + 69.3 A$_{\overline{2}|0.16}$ (1.16)$^{-3}$
−53.361 A$_{\overline{2}|0.16}$ (1.16)$^{-4}$
−22 − 85.35 + 40.88 + 191.80
−137.32 + 71.27
− 47.31 = +11.97 NPV

State E −22 −99(1.16)$^{-1}$ +55(1.16)$^{-2}$ +2970 A$_{\overline{5}|0.16}$ (1.16)$^{-1}$
−2286.9 A$_{\overline{5}|0.16}$ (1.16)$^{-2}$ + 1485 A$_{\overline{5}|0.16}$ (1.16)$^{-6}$
−1143 A$_{\overline{5}|0.16}$ (1.16)$^{-7}$
−22 − 85.35 + 40.88 + 8383.64
−5565.08 + 1964.37
−1324.10 = +3892.86 NPV

Expected NPV

£m NPV	×	Probability		
−12.52	×	0.50	=	− 6.26
−17.42	×	0.35	=	− 6.10
−66.47	×	0.09	=	− 5.98
+11.97	×	0.048	=	+ 0.57
+3892.86	×	0.012	=	+ 46.71

$$\text{+£28.94m ENPV}$$

(b) *Revised probability tree*
    The revised probability tree is shown in Fig. 11.1. The survey

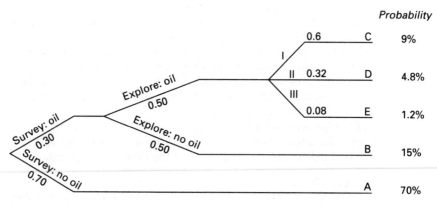

Figure 11.1

only changes the probabilities of states A and B. Therefore its
worth should be determined by the difference the change in probabilities makes to the ENPV of these two outcomes, plus the cost
of the existing survey:

State	NPV £m	×	Existing Probability			State	NPV £m	×	Revised Probability		
A	−12.52	×	0.50	=	− 6.26	A	−12.52	×	0.70	=	− 8.76
B	−17.42	×	0.35	=	− 6.10	B	−17.42	×	0.15	=	− 2.61
			ENPV		−12.36				ENPV		−11.37

The difference between is:

$$
\begin{array}{ll}
& \text{£m} \\
& 12.36 \\
& \underline{11.37} \\
& 0.99 \\
\text{Plus cost of existing survey:} & 2.00 \\
\text{Less PV of tax relief:} & \underline{(0.86)} \quad = \quad \text{£2.0m} \times 0.50 \times (1.16)^{-1} \\
& \underline{\text{£2.13m}} \quad = \quad \text{Max } \textit{after-tax} \text{ value of new survey}
\end{array}
$$

Let X = gross cost of the new survey, then:

$$X - X \times 0.50 \times (1.16)^{-1} = 2.13$$
$$0.569X = 2.13$$
$$X = 2.13/0.569 = \underline{\underline{\text{£3.74m (approx.)}}}$$

Answer to problem 2

(a) The market research cost has already been incurred and so can be ignored for decision purposes.

NPV analysis
Outlay   £200,000
Revenue   £250,000 per year
Variable costs   £150,000 per year
Fixed costs   £25,000 per year
Scrap value   £2,000
Life   4 years
Discount rate   10%

$$
\left.
\begin{array}{l}
-200 + (250 - 150 - 25)\ A_{\overline{4}|\,0.10} + 2(1.10)^{-4} \\
-200 + (75 \times 3.1699) + (2 \times 0.6830)
\end{array}
\right\} = \underline{+\text{£39,108 NPV}}
$$

$$\therefore \text{ accept}$$

Sensitivity analysis
Let outlay = X

$$-X + 75\ A_{\overline{4}|\,0.10} + 2(1.10)^{-4} = 0 \text{ NPV}$$
$$-X = -75\ A_{\overline{4}|\,0.10} - 2(1.10)^{-4} = \underline{-\text{£239,108}}$$

% change: $\dfrac{239,108 - 200,000}{200,000} = \underline{0.196}$

Let revenue = X

$$-200 + X \, A_{\overline{4}|0.10} - 175 \, A_{\overline{4}|0.10} + 2(1.10)^{-4} = 0$$

$$X = \frac{200 + 175 \, A_{\overline{4}|0.10} - 2(1.10)^{-4}}{A_{\overline{4}|0.10}} = \underline{£237{,}662}$$

% change: $\dfrac{250{,}000 - 237{,}662}{250{,}000} = \underline{0.049}$

Let variable costs = X

$$-200 + 250 \, A_{\overline{4}|0.10} - X \, A_{\overline{4}|0.10} - 25 \, A_{\overline{4}|0.10} + 2(1.10)^{-4} = 0$$

$$-X = \frac{200 - 250 \, A_{\overline{4}|0.10} + 25 \, A_{\overline{4}|0.10} - 2(1.10)^{-4}}{A_{\overline{4}|0.10}} = \underline{-£162{,}337}$$

% change: $\dfrac{162{,}337 - 150{,}000}{150{,}000} = \underline{0.082}$

Let fixed costs = X

$$-200 + 250 \, A_{\overline{4}|0.10} - 150 \, A_{\overline{4}|0.10} - X \, A_{\overline{4}|0.10} + 2(1.10)^{-4} = 0$$

$$-X = \frac{200 - 250 \, A_{\overline{4}|0.10} + 150 \, A_{\overline{4}|0.10} - 2(1.10)^{-4}}{A_{\overline{4}|0.10}} = \underline{-£37{,}337}$$

% change: $\dfrac{37{,}337 - 25{,}000}{25{,}000} = \underline{0.494}$

Let life = X years

$$-200 + 75 \, A_{\overline{X}|0.10} + 2(1.10)^{-X} = 0$$

When $X = 4$ NPV = +£39,108
When $X = 2$ NPV = $-200 + (75 \times 1.7355) + (2 \times 0.8264) = \underline{-£68{,}185}$

$$X = 2 + \left[\frac{-68185}{-68185 - 39108} \times (4 - 2) \right] = \underline{3.27 \text{ years}}$$

% change: $\dfrac{4 - 3.27}{4} = \underline{0.182}$

Let sales price = X

$$-200 + 50X \, A_{\overline{4}|0.10} - 175 \, A_{\overline{4}|0.10} + 2(1.10)^{-4} = 0$$

$$X = \frac{200 + 175 \ A_{\overline{4}|0.10} - 2(1.10)^{-4}}{50 \ A_{\overline{4}|0.10}} = \underline{\underline{£4.75}}$$

% change: $\dfrac{£5 - £4.75}{£5} = \underline{0.05}$

Let sales volume $= X$

$$-200 + (5 - 3)X \ A_{\overline{4}|0.10} - 25 \ A_{\overline{4}|0.10} + 2(1.10)^{-4} = 0$$

$$X = \frac{200 + 25 \ A_{\overline{4}|0.10} - 2(1.10)^{-4}}{(5 - 3) \ A_{\overline{4}|0.10}} = \underline{\underline{43{,}831 \ \text{bottles}}}$$

% change: $\dfrac{50{,}000 - 43{,}831}{43{,}831} = \underline{0.123}$

Let variable cost/bottle $= X$

$$-200 + 250 \ A_{\overline{4}|0.10} - 50X \ A_{\overline{4}|0.10} - 25 \ A_{\overline{4}|0.10} + 2(1.10)^{-4} = 0$$

$$X = \frac{200 - 250 \ A_{\overline{4}|0.10} + 25 \ A_{\overline{4}|0.10} + 2(1.10)^{-4}}{50 \ A_{\overline{4}|0.10}} = \underline{\underline{£3.25}}$$

% change: $\dfrac{£3.25 - £3}{£3} = \underline{0.083}$

(b) *Sensitivity Table*

Forecast	Max % change
Outlay	19.6% rise
Revenue	4.9% fall
Variable cost	8.2% rise
Fixed cost	49.4% rise
Life	18.2% fall
Sales price	5.0% fall
Sales volume	12.3% fall
Variable cost/unit	8.3% rise

The sensitivity table indicates that the 'accept' advice given by the NPV analysis is most sensitive to changes in the estimates of the annual revenue and the sales price. Management should go back and ensure that they cannot significantly improve their confidence in the reliability of both estimates.

(c)   Expected Year 6 sales:

$$
\begin{array}{lrcr}
\text{Successful:} & 28{,}000 \times 0.5 & = & 14{,}000 \\
 & 9{,}000 \times 0.5 & = & \underline{4{,}500} \\
 & & & 18{,}500 \\[4pt]
\text{Unsuccessful:} & 12{,}000 \times 0.5 & = & 6{,}000 \\
 & 5{,}000 \times 0.5 & = & \underline{2{,}500} \\
 & & & 8{,}500
\end{array}
$$

Contribution/sale: £5 − £3 = £2

ENPV of contribution (£000s)

5	6		PV		Probability
$+70(1.10)^{-5}$	$+37(1.10)^{-6}$	=	64,350	× 0.6 =	38,610
$+14(1.10)^{-5}$	$+17(1.10)^{-6}$	=	18,289	× 0.4 =	$\underline{7{,}316}$
					+45,926

PV of fixed costs (£000s)

$$-25(1.10)^{-5} \qquad -25(1.10)^{-6} = -29{,}635$$

Therefore the PV of the life extention would be:

$$£45{,}926 - £29{,}635 = +£16{,}291$$

PV cost of trade advertising (£000s)

$$-10(1.10)^{-5} -10(1.10)^{-6} = -11{,}854$$

PV cost of price reduction (£000s)

$$
\begin{array}{l}
-35 \times 0.40(1.10)^{-5} - 18.5 \times 0.40(1.10)^{-6} = -12{,}870 \times 0.6 = -7{,}722 \\
-\ 7 \times 0.40(1.10)^{-5} -\ \ 8.5 \times 0.40(1.10)^{-6} = -3{,}658 \ \times 0.4 = \underline{-1{,}463} \\
\hspace{9cm} -9{,}185
\end{array}
$$

NPV of life extention with trade advertising

$$£16{,}291 - £11{,}854 = +£4{,}437$$

NPV of life extention with price reduction:

$$£16{,}291 - £9{,}185 = +£7{,}106$$

Therefore, although either alternative would be worthwhile, the 'price reduction' alternative leads to the largest additional amount of positive NPV.

Answer to problem 3

(a) *Report*

Assuming that the investment in Goer is undertaken, is it better to continue with the project at the end of the first year, or to abandon it?

If it is decided *not* to abandon the project at Year 1, there is an opportunity cost of £141,000 – the payment from Goer that is foregone.

In Year 2, there are four possible outcomes: a cash flow of £80,000, £90,000, £100,000 or £110,000, plus £81,000 'final' payment.

The NPV of deciding *not* to abandon at Year 1 is as follows:

Year 1 cash flow: £80,000

Year 1	Year 2	NPV at 18%		Prob.		
(141,000)	80,000 } 81,000	(3867)	×	0.6	=	(2,320)
(141,000)	90,000 } 81,000	3314	×	0.4	=	1,326
				ENPV		(994)

Year 1 cash flow: £100,000

Year 1	Year 2	NPV at 18%		Prob.		
(141,000)	100,000 } 81,000	10497	×	0.6	=	6,298
(141,000)	110,000 } 81,000	17679	×	0.4	=	7,072
				ENPV		13,370

Therefore if, at the end of Year 1, the company receives a cash flow of £80,000, the best course of action is then to *abandon* the project, (for to continue incurs a negative ENPV of £994). However, if at the end of Year 1, the company receives a cash flow of £100,000, the best course of action is to *continue* the project (for continuing generates a positive ENPV of £13,370).

Now that the optimal action at Year 1 is known, the overall investment decision can be evaluated.

There are three possible 'states of the world'. State I is where the company receives a £80,000 cash inflow at Year 1 and so abandons the project. The probability of this state is 0.60.

State II is where the company receives a £100,000 cash inflow at Year 1, continues with the project and receives another

£100,000 cash inflow at Year 2. The probability of this state is: 0.40 × 0.60 = 0.24.

State III is where the company receives a £100,000 cash inflow at Year 1, continues with the project and receives a £110,000 cash inflow at Year 2. The probability of this state is: 0.40 × 0.40 = 0.16.

NPV analysis

State	Year 0	Year 1	Year 2	NPV at 18%		Probability		
I	(201,000)	80,000 } 141,000		(13702)	×	0.6	=	(8221)
II	(201,000)	100,000	100,000 } 81,000	13744	×	0.24	=	3299
III	(201,000)	100,000	110,000 } 81,000	20926	×	0.16	=	3348
						ENPV		£(1574)

Therefore, despite the abandonment option at Year 1, the overall project is *not* worthwhile. The company would do better to invest its £20,000 in the money market which represents a zero NPV investment.

(b) The practical problems of abandonment analysis relate primarily to the estimation of the relevant cash flows. It is difficult, if not impossible to accurately estimate:
   (i)   Annual net cash flows. Cash flows are usually estimated to be single figures, e.g. £80,000 or £100,000, whereas in reality they might take various alternative values.
   (ii) The conditional probabilities associated with the cash flows.
   (iii) The actual abandonment value. Unless contractual agreements exist, the abandonment value estimated may be subject to substantial error.
Estimates of NPV are likely to be less accurate as the number of years that an abandonment opportunity exists increases.

Abandonment is normally advocated in the first year that the present value of abandonment exceeds the present value of expected cash flows from continued operation. However, abandonment at a later date might produce an even greater expected present value. The normal abandonment rule might lead, therefore, to a sub-optimal decision.

Abandonment part-way through the expected economic life might occur for many reasons, which result in the present value of abandonment exceeding the expected present value of continuing. Important factors might include unexpected unfavourable changes in inflation, exchange rates, taxation, labour, material and other costs, the development of new technology, labour disputes and increased competition.

Answer to problem 4

(a)   Choice of initial production capacity: The *fixed* costs of setting up production can be ignored here.

Contribution/Unit: £500 − £400 = £100
Valuable Set-Up Costs/Unit = £50

32,000 production capacity

	Sales	Contribution £000s		Probability		
(OPT)	32,000	3,200	×	0.2	=	640
(BG)	16,000	1,600	×	0.5	=	800
(PESS)	4,000	400	×	0.3	=	120

1560 Expected Year 1 contribution
Less variable set-up costs: 32,000 × £50 =   (1600)

(40) Expected net cash flow

16,000 production capacity

	Sales	Contribution £000s		Probability		
(OPT)	16,000	1,600	×	0.2	=	320
(BG)	16,000	1,600	×	0.5	=	800
(PESS)	4,000	400	×	0.3	=	120

1240 Expected Year 1 contribution
Less variable set-up costs: 16,000 × £50 =   (800)

400 Expected net cash flow

4,000 production capacity

	Sales	Contribution £000s		Probability		
(OPT)	4,000	400	×	0.2	=	80
(BG)	4,000	400	×	0.5	=	200
(PESS)	4,000	400	×	0.3	=	120

400 Expected Year 1 contribution
Less variable set-up costs: 4,000 × £50 =   (200)

200 Expected net cash flow

Therefore the production capacity which gives the best 'Year 1' expected net cash flow is 16,000 units.

ENPV of 16,000 production capacity (£000s)

Year 1   Expected contribution (see above): £1,240

Year 2   Expected contribution 1600 × 0.2 = 320
                                800 × 0.5 = 400   £780
                                200 × 0.3 = 60

Year 3   Expected contribution 1200 × 0.2 = 240
                                600 × 0.5 = 300   £585
                                150 × 0.3 = 45

Year	Cash flow expected £000s	Discount factor		P.V. cash flow
0	(1800)	×	1	= (1800)
1	1240	×	0.9091	= 1127.3
2	780	×	0.8264	= 644.6
3	585	×	0.7513	= 439.5
				+£414.40 ENPV

(b)   Survey indicates 'most optimistic' sales level: 32,000 production capacity installed. Resulting NPV:

Year	Cash flow expected £000s	Discount factor		P.V. cash flow
0	(2600)	×	1	= (2600)
1	3200	×	0.9091	= 2909.1
2	1600	×	0.8264	= 1322.2
3	1200	×	0.7513	= 901.6
				+£2532.9 NPV

Survey indicates 'best guess' sales levels: 16,000 installed. Resulting NPV:

Year	Cash flow expected £000s	Discount factor		P.V. cash flow
0	(1800)	×	1	= (1800)
1	1600	×	0.9091	= 1454.6
2	800	×	0.8264	= 661.1
3	600	×	0.7513	= 450.8
				+£766.5 NPV

Survey indicates 'most pessimistic' sales level: 4,000 production capacity installed. Resulting NPV:

Year	Cash flow expected £000s		Discount factor		P.V. cash flow	
0	(1200)	×	1	=	(1200)	As this results
1	400	×	0.9091	=	363.6	in a *negative*
2	200	×	0.8264	=	165.3	NPV, company
3	150	×	0.7513	=	112.7	would *not*
					−£558,4 NPV	undertake
						project

Survey results	NPV		Prob.		
Optimistic	+2532.9	×	0.2	=	506.6
Best guess	+ 766.5	×	0.5	=	383.2
Pessimistic	0	×	0.3	=	0
					+£889,800 ENPV

ENPV with survey	£889,800
ENPV without survey	£414,400
Added value of survey	£475,400
Cost of survey	£300,000
Excess worth	£175,400

Hence survey is worthwhile

Expected value calculation have three main limitations as an aid to corporate decision making.

(i)   Provide an arithmetic mean outcome figure which has a very limited interpretation where one-off business investment decisions are concerned and the dispersion of outcomes is likely to be of just as much interest to decision makers to give an appreciation of the risk involved with the decision.

(ii) The arithmetic mean outcome figure loses even more meaning when the dispersion of outcomes is skewed, as is the case here.

(iii) The probabilities used are 'subjective', not 'classical' and simply reflect the decision maker's own judgement.

(c) Most business decision making is undertaken within a highly uncertain world. Some of this uncertainty can be reduced by spending more time, effort and money on gathering additional information.

However, information, like any other good, has a maximum worth equal to the sum of the benefits received from its possession. Thus *additional* information is worthwhile only if its expected benefits exceed the expected cost. In the case in question, this is precisely the situation and so the research information is worth having.

However, in the question, the survey was assumed to be error-free. In the real world, most market research surveys would be open to various types of error and bias and it may well be difficult to allow for this in any ex ante evaluation of the information's potential worth.

12
The cost of company capital

Answer to problem 1

(a) (i) Price/share = 35.8p × 28 = 1,002.4p

Dividend growth rate = $(11 \div 4.86)^{1/4} - 1 = \underline{22.7\%}$

Cost of equity capital = $\dfrac{11(1 + 0.227)}{1,002.4} + 0.227 = \underline{\underline{24\%}}$

(ii) Proportion of retained earnings: $\dfrac{35.8 - 11}{35.8} = \underline{0.693}$

Return on capital employed: $\dfrac{35.8}{190} = \underline{0.188}$

∴ Dividend growth rate = 0.693 × 0.188 = $\underline{13\%}$

Cost of equity capital = $\dfrac{11(1 + 0.13)}{1,002.4} + 0.13 = \underline{\underline{14.2\%}}$

(iii) Cost of equity capital = 10% + [9% × 0.80] = $\underline{17.2\%}$

(b) The dividend growth model used contains three principal assumptions:

(i)   shares are valued on the basis of the present value sum of future expected dividends;

(ii) the share price used is in equilibrium;

(iii) the estimated dividend growth rate will continue indefinitely.

The first of these assumptions could be assumed to be reasonably realistic. The second assumption is, however, open to some doubt, as the company's P/E multiple is substantially different from the average of what is a reasonably homogenous industry group. Nevertheless, the most serious doubts concern the third assumption. Forecasting the future on the basis of what has occurred in the past is never satisfactory unless there are positive reasons to believe that the past will replicate itself in the future. In this case this may be particularly unrealistic, given that the company has achieved a very high rate of dividend growth in the recent past.

It is doubtful whether such a trend would be maintained indefinitely.

The 'Gordon' model also makes three specific assumptions:

(i)   the proportion of retained earnings and the company's ROCE remain constant in the future;
(ii)   the company is all-equity financed;
(iii) projects are only financed out of retained earnings.

In the example in question, although the retention rate has remained reasonably constant over the recent past, the firm's ROCE has changed significantly, growing steadily from 15.6% to 18.8%. Thus doubt must be cast on the realism of the assumption that this will remain constant in the future.

As far as the second assumption is concerned, Thamos is indeed all-equity financed at present – but it may not necessarily remain so in the future. The third assumption also holds at present, but again it may be unrealistic to assume that the firm will not wish to raise additional equity finance at some future point in time.

It is because of the questionable nature of some of the assumptions which lie behind these models that it is not surprising that the two estimates of future dividend growth, approximately 23% and 13%, are so different. This, in turn, then feeds through into the estimate of the cost of equity capital.

Finally, the CAPM-based estimate of the company's cost of equity capital is also founded on a number of assumptions, the realism of which might be open to question. Principal amongst these would be:

(i)   beta is the sole determinant of return;
(ii)   tax has been correctly taken into account;
(iii) the risk-free return and the market risk premium have been correctly identified;
(iv)   investors have homogeneous expectations and a one-period time horizon;
(v)   betas are stable over time.

These, and many other assumptions behind the CAPM, are of questionable real-world validity. However, the real question concerning the applicability of CAPM to generate a firm's cost of equity capital is: Is it empirically valid and does it work in practice? Although this evidence has come in for recent criticism, the best-known study of this question is by Black, Jensen and Scholes (1972) which does tend to suggest that the CAPM is, at least approximately, correct in relation to reality – although it may be that the model is just too simplistic and a model using multi-factor determinants of return may be more applicable to the real world.

In many ways the three models used are not competitors, but just take different views of the same problem. However, given the data input difficulties that are associated with all the models, it is not surprising that the diversity of results obtained in part (a) has actually occurred.

(c)   In pure finance theory, it is highly debatable whether managers do need to know their firm's cost of equity capital and, in practice, many managers may well believe that cost of capital numbers produced as in part (a) owe more to fiction than reality.

It is conceivable that a company operating in a single area of business and wishing to evaluate an investment project that is in that same area, may require knowledge of the cost of equity capital as an input into the weighted average cost of capital (WACC) computation, in order to obtain a discount rate. Additionally, a manager might also want to identify the company's cost of equity capital as an input into a WACC calculation in an attempt to observe the effect on the WACC (and on the cost of equity) of a change in the company's capital structure (see Chapter 13).

However, perhaps the most useful information imparted to managers by a company's cost of equity capital is its opportunity cost implications. The cost of equity capital represents the return available to shareholders, elsewhere on the capital markets, from an investment of a similar level of risk to that of investing in the company's shares. Thus it could be interpreted as being the minimum return that management should earn on investing shareholders' funds. As an investment criterion, this has only a restricted validity because the risk level has to be held constant. However, it does have the advantage of clearly bringing home to management the fact that retained earnings – forming as they do part of shareholders' funds – cannot be considered 'costless' or 'free' capital, but have a very significant opportunity cost.

Answer to problem 2

(a)   Given the information, the estimates of the cost of capital can be found from using the dividend valuation model:

$$K_E = \frac{d_0(1 + g)}{P_E} + g$$

where g can either be estimated from the past rate of growth of dividends (i); or on the basis of Gordon's approach, where $g = b \times r$ (ii).

Black Snake
(i) $2473 (1 + g)^5 = 6158$

$$g = (6158 \div 2473)^{1/5} - 1 = \underline{0.20}$$

$$K_E = \frac{4.11(1 + 0.20)}{342} + 0.20 = \underline{\underline{21.4\%}}$$

(ii) $\quad b = \dfrac{56700}{62858} = 0.90 \quad r = \dfrac{62858}{315000} = 0.20$

$g = 0.90 \times 0.20 = \underline{0.18}$

$K_E = \dfrac{4.11(1 + 0.18)}{342} + 0.18 = \underline{\underline{19.4\%}}$

White Turkey
(i) $\quad 372 \, (1 + g)^5 = 599$

$g = (599 \div 372)^{1/5} - 1 = \underline{0.10}$

$K_E = \dfrac{29.95(1 + 0.10)}{220} + 0.10 = \underline{\underline{24.9\%}}$

(ii) $\quad b = \dfrac{390}{989} = 0.39 \quad r = \dfrac{989}{3800} = 0.26$

$g = 0.39 \times 0.26 = \underline{0.1025}$

$K_E = \dfrac{29.95(1 + 0.1025)}{220} + 0.1025 = \underline{\underline{25.3\%}}$

Red Eagle
(i) $\quad 7122 \, (1 + g)^5 = 11466$

$g = (11466 \div 7122)^{1/5} - 1 = \underline{0.10}$

$K_e = \dfrac{11.47(1 + 0.10)}{149} + 0.10 = \underline{\underline{18.5\%}}$

(ii) $\quad b = \dfrac{10530}{21996} = 0.48 \quad r = \dfrac{21996}{117000} = 0.188$

$g = 0.48 \times 0.188 = \underline{0.09}$

$K_e = \dfrac{11.47(1 + 0.09)}{149} + 0.09 = \underline{\underline{17.4\%}}$

(b) The equity cost of capital is normally defined as the rate of return required by the ordinary shareholders of a company and this rate is a function of risk, given that the investor is risk-averse.

The risk element of the cost of capital can be of two types: financial and business (see Chapter 14). Financial risk reflects the uncertainty in the receipt of future dividends arising from gearing and, as all the companies are equity financed, this particular aspect of risk is not relevant to the analysis. However, business risk will be an important determinant of the cost of capital, as it defines expectations as to the future variability of the operating income of the business and this factor is central in analysing variations in the cost of capital estimates.

The six companies appear to fall into three groups, as follows:

Group 1 Red Fox and Red Eagle $k_e \simeq 18\%$
Group 2 White Turkey and White Eyes $k_e \simeq 25\%$
Group 3 Black Snake and Black Stump $k_e \simeq 20\%$

Group 1 comprises the two diversified companies and, given that the cost of capital is positively related to cash flow variability, it is significant that the two companies with the greatest range of business activities have the lowest cost of capital. This is due to the favourable effects of diversification where the portfolio of projects represents an effective 'hedge' against uncertainty.

The 'hedge' is created by selecting projects which are less than perfectly positively correlated with the cash flows from existing projects. The nearer the correlation coefficient is to -1, the greater the reduction in risk of the project combination. The structure of the diversified companies could therefore be a major determinant of their lower cost of capital rates. It should be noted, however, that risk is commonly a combination of systematic and unsystematic risk. The former arises from the holding of all assets and it is not possible to diversify against it. Unsystematic risk is inherent in the nature of the asset itself and this portion of 'total risk' can be reduced by diversification.

This leaves unexplained the difference in the cost of capital for the non-diversified companies. On the assumption that the capital market is reasonably efficient, market forces should prevent share prices of companies in the same risk class from indicating different rates of return. Possible explanations could be.

(i)   As a result of the relatively few issued shares in both White Turkey and White Eyes, there could be marketability problems in terms of fluidity of trading. This kind of imperfection therefore tends to increase the required rate of return due to the uncertainty regarding future opportunities for buying and selling the securities.

(ii) Although all four firms are in the brewing industry, investors may be making different estimates of the business risk of the companies. This can be justified by assuming that risk is based on more specific variables than a broad industrial classification. The expectations of the market may be influenced by attitudes towards factors such as management ability, product diversification, strategic flexibility and access to funds.

(iii) Black Snake and Black Stump are by far the larger companies, and the market may well be associating a certain degree of risk with corporate size and so demanding an additional premium from the smaller firms. Again, this may be related to portfolio effects.

(c) Additional information which would be likely to raise confidence in the cost of capital estimates might include the following:
  (i) actual details of earnings and dividends during the previous five years;
  (ii) future projections of both earnings and dividends, together with any information on future plans and projects;
  (iii) comparative data on other companies in the same industrial sectors;
  (iv) historic records of share transactions;
  (v) details of diversification within the companies and the market relationships between different products and activities;
  (vi) a closer examination of the capital employed data, with particular reference to the current value of the assets;
  (vii) details of previous capital retention policies.

Answer to problem 3

The 'true worth' of a company could be said to be equal to the present value sum of the future expected cash flow that the company can be expected to generate. This cash flow includes not only that which the company's existing investments (and management) are able to generate, but also those generated by the growth opportunities available to the firm.

In contrast, the market value of a share represents the sum of the future expected dividend flow that is expected to accrue to the share, discounted to present value. Thus the market price simply reflects the cost (on a 'per share' basis) of a marginal – i.e. non-controlling – investment in the company. The market capitalization of a company is then simply the product of its 'per share' market value and the number of shares in issue. As such, the market capitalization has very little meaning: the stock market places a value on the individual share, not on all the shares in aggregate.

However, if the stock market believes that there may be a party interested in buying the entire equity capital – including the asset of 'control' – then it will attempt to reflect the company's 'true worth' in the market capitalization. In other words, in such circumstances the market does then value all the shares in aggregate, and the 'per share' market price is then derived by dividing this figure by the number of shares in issue.

Therefore the true worth of a company *may* be reflected in the market capitalization figure, but only in circumstances where there is the possibility of a take-over of the whole company. Using the figures in the question as an example, Clorinda's equity market capitalization is currently £7.3m and this simply reflects the per share value given by the market. However, if a more dynamic management were to be installed, the resulting rationalization, together with the realization of unused (or under-used) assets might well indicate a true worth for the company of £11.7m + £1.2m = £12.9m. Given an efficient market, once the stock market becomes aware of Berenice's interest, the market price may well move to approximately this figure (or to whatever figure does represent the market's best estimate of the company's true worth).

Another factor to consider in the specific case of Clorinda which may also result in a divergence between true worth and the market capitalization concerns the efficiency of the stock market. Given the relatively small size of Clorinda, together with a relatively limited number of shareholders, there may be little trading activity in the company's shares. In such circumstances, the lack of liquidity may cause the market price of the company's equity – and hence the market capitalization of the company – to diverge even from being equal to the present value sum of the future expected dividend flow.

13
The weighted average cost of capital

Answer to problem 1

(a) *Cost of equity capital*

$$K_E = \frac{d_0(1 + g)}{P_E} + g \qquad \text{where } P_E = 135 \text{ p}$$
$$g = (13.6 - 10)^{1/4} - 1 = 0.08$$
$$d_0 = 13.6 \text{ p}$$

$$\therefore K_E = \frac{13.6(1 + 0.08)}{135} + 0.08 = \underline{0.189},$$

Cost of debentures

$V_D = £800,000 \times 0.825 = £660,000$

K_D is found by solving:

$$+£82.50 - £8 \cdot A_{\overline{4}| K_D} - £100(1 + K_D)^{-4} = 0$$

Using linear interpolation:

At 10%: $+ 82.50 - 8 \cdot A_{\overline{4}|0.10} - 100(1 + 0.10)^{-4} = -11.16$

At 16%: $+ 82.50 - 8 \cdot A_{\overline{4}|0.16} - 100(1 + 0.16)^{-4} = + 4.88$

$$\therefore K_D \approx 10\% + \left\{ \frac{-11.16}{-11.16 - 4.88} \times 6\% \right\} = \underline{0.142}$$

Cost of bank loan

As the interest rate is variable with market rate movements:

$V_L = £900,000$

$K_L = \underline{0.165}$

Weighted average cost of capital (K_0)

$$K_0 = \frac{V_E \cdot K_E + V_D \cdot K_D + V_L \cdot K_L}{V_E + V_D + V_L}$$

where

$$V_E = \text{£}1.35 \times 3\text{m} = \text{£}4.05\text{m} \quad K_E = 18.9\%$$
$$V_D = \text{£}0.66\text{m} \quad\quad\quad\quad\quad\quad K_D = 14.2\%$$
$$V_L = \text{£}0.9\text{m} \quad\quad\quad\quad\quad\quad\ K_L = 16.5\%$$

$$\therefore K_0 = \frac{(4.05 \times 18.9) + (0.66 + 14.2) + (0.9 + 16.5\%)}{4.05 + 0.66 + 0.9} = \underline{18\%}$$

(b)   Apart from the obvious assumptions that the market values and the costs of capital used in the calculation of the WACC are correct, there are three major assumptions that have to be made if the WACC is to be a reliable discount rate for project appraisal. They are:

(i)   the project is marginal;
(ii)   the company will maintain its existing gearing ratio;
(iii) the project has the same degree of (systematic) risk as the company's existing cash flows.

The project should be marginal (i.e. small relative to the size of the firm) because the WACC is a marginal cost of capital figure. It is so because each of the individual costs of capital that go up to make the WACC are themselves marginal costs of capital. For example, the cost of equity capital of (approximately) 19% represents the return that the market would require from a marginal (i.e. relatively small) investment in the company's equity. Thus the WACC is an appropriate discount rate or minimum required rate of return for a relatively small capital investment project.

As can be seen in the calculation of the WACC in part (a) above, it is based on the company's existing capital structure (gearing ratio). If the company were to change its gearing, then the WACC could be expected to change also, for two reasons. First, changing the gearing would change the weights applied to the individual costs of capital, and second, changing the gearing would also change the degree of financial risk held by ordinary shareholders and would thus, in turn, change the cost of equity capital. Only in a Modigliani and Miller world of no taxes and perfect markets would this assumption prove unnecessary (see Chapter 14).

Finally, the company's WACC relates to the degree of risk surrounding the company's existing cash flows. Therefore it would be appropriate to use this as an investment appraisal discount rate only if the investment project has a similar level of risk.

(c) A number of practical problems are likely to be encountered in the calculation of real world WACCs. However, there are three principal problems.

The first is that capital structures are often far more complex in practice than in textbook examples/calculations, with some securities causing really difficult valuation problems. Examples would include convertible debentures, loan stocks in foreign currencies (Eurobonds, etc.) and unquoted, fixed-interest capital.

The second problem specifically concerns the calculation of the cost of equity capital. To obtain this number, estimates are normally required of the market value of the equity and of the future dividend growth rate. With the market value of the equity there is a problem in deciding what value to take if the share price is relatively volatile, but the real problem concerns the dividend growth rate estimate. The past dividend growth rate may be highly erratic, or it might have been depressed because of legal restraints on dividends, or it may be non-existent in the sense that no dividends have been paid in recent years. In all cases, estimating the future dividend growth rate becomes highly problematical. The Gordon approach (where the growth rate $g = b \times r$) may be of some help in such circumstances, but again it is hedged around by a number of assumptions such as constant earnings retention percentages and constant rates of return on reinvested earnings which severely limit its usefulness. One other approach to calculating the cost of equity capital would be to use the capital asset pricing model rather than the dividend valuation model, but that too has its operational difficulties, in particular the specification of the risk-free interest rate and the rate of return on the overall market.

The final major problem with the real-world calculation of WACC is caused by taxation. In a taxed world what is required is an after-tax WACC, but the corporate tax regime is now so complex and specific in terms of how it affects individual companies, that major problems are posed in trying to arrive at a reliable after-tax WACC estimate.

Answer to problem 2

(a) (i) *Equity capital*

$K_E = \underline{18\%}$ (given)

$V_E = $ 8m $\times$ £1.10 $= \underline{£8.8m}$

(ii) *Irredeemable debentures*

$$K_{IRR} = \frac{\text{Annual Int. } (1 - T_c)}{\text{Mkt. value, ex. int.}} = \frac{£3(1 - 0.35)}{£31.60 - £3} = \frac{1.95}{28.6} = \underline{0.068}$$

$V_{IRR} = $ £1.4m $\times$ 0.286 $= \underline{£0.4004m}$

(iii) *Redeemable debentures*

K_{RED}, is found by solving the internal rate of return of the following cash flow:

$$(£103.26 - £9) - 9(1 - 0.35)A_{\overline{10}|K_{RED}} - £100(1 + K_{RED})^{-10} = 0$$

At 10% discount rate NPV = +19.76

At 4% discount rate NPV = −20.75

Interpolating:

$$K_{RED} \simeq 4\% + \left\{ \frac{-20.75}{-20.75 - 19.76} \times (10\% - 4\%) \right\} = \underline{7.07\%}$$

$V_{RED} = £1.5m \times 0.9426 = \underline{£1.4139m}$

(iv) *Loan stock*

Current value of each £100 unit of loan stock:

$$£6 \, A_{\overline{10}| \, 0.10} + £100(1 + 0.10)^{-10} = £75.42$$

$V_L = £2m \times 0.7542 = \underline{£1.5084m}$

K_L is found by solving the IRR of the following cash flow:

$$+£75.84 - £6(1 - 0.35)A_{\overline{10}| \, K_L} - £100(1 + K_L)^{-10} = 0$$

At 4% discount rate NPV = −23.35

At 10% discount rate NPV = +13.32

Interpolating:

$$K_L \simeq 4\% + \left\{ \frac{-23.35}{-23.35 - 13.32} \times (10\% - 4\%) \right\} = \underline{7.82\%}$$

(v) *Bank loans*

$K_B = 13\%(1 - 0.35) = \underline{8.45\%}$
$V_B = \underline{£1.54m}$

(vi) *Weighted average cost of capital (WACC)*

$K_0 = \{(18\% \times 8.8) + (6.8\% \times 0.4004) + (7.04\% \times 1.4139)$
$\quad + (7.82\% \times 1.5084) + (8.45\% \times 1.54)\}/\{(8.8$
$\quad + 0.4004 + 1.4139 + 1.5084 + 1.54)\}$

$$K_0 = \frac{195.93}{13.66} = \underline{\underline{14.3\%}}$$

(b)   In order to estimate a company's weighted average cost of capital it is necessary to estimate the after-tax market return and market capitalization (or equivalent) of each type of long-term capital. Thus in judging the difficulty encountered with any one particular type of capital, both aspects should be taken into account.

      The presence of bank overdrafts in the capital structure do not cause much difficulty as long as the amount of the overdraft remains reasonably stable. The interest rate charged on the overdraft can be expected to vary with changes in market interest rates and so the current 'market value' of the overdraft will remain equal to its nominal amount. Furthermore, given that the overdraft is repaid at par, the after-tax market return will simply be the current actual overdraft interest rate, adjusted for the tax relief on the interest payments.

      Convertible loan stock causes greater difficulties. Such stock may well have a market quotation, and in such circumstances finding its capitalized market value causes no problems. However, if it is unquoted an equivalent valuation must be estimated. The valuation of this type of security can be approached by splitting it into two elements, the loan stock itself and the convertible option, which is a call option on the company's equity. Thus its market value can be estimated as whichever is the greater between its value as a simple loan stock and its value if converted immediately, plus the value of the call option.

      Apart from these difficulties, whether or not a market value exists, there is still the problem of estimating the market return on the security, which requires the determination of the point in time at which conversion is expected to take place, and the expected gain that the stockholders can be expected to make upon conversion.

(c)   There are four fundamental assumptions that are made when a company's weighted average cost of capital (WACC) is used as an NPV discount rate. These are:

  (i)   the project under evaluation is marginal;

 (ii)   the project, if accepted, is financed in such a way as not to change the company's existing capital structure;

(iii)   level perpetuity cash flows;

(iv)   the project has the same degree of systematic risk as the company's existing projects.

The assumption that the project should be marginal, i.e. that it is small relative to the size of the company is necessary because the WACC itself is a marginal rate of return. The WACC is made up of the 'cost' of each individual source of the company's capital, and each of these costs represents the required return on a marginal investment in that security. For example, the company's cost of equity capital represents the required market return for a marginal investment in the company's equity. Hence the WACC should only be applied to evaluating relatively small capital investment projects.

      The second assumption is required (except in an Modigliani

Miller world with no taxation) because a change in the company's captial structure can be expected to change its WACC. There are two reasons for this. Firstly, changing the gearing ratio will change the amount of financial risk borne by ordinary shareholders and hence will change the 'cost of equity capital' value in the WACC calculation, and secondly, changing the gearing will in turn change the weights (assuming market value weights) used in the WACC calculation.

The third fundamental assumption arises from the fact that, strictly speaking, the WACC calculation is a level perpetuity model. Hence the different types of company capital should involve only level perpetuity cash flows, as so too should the cash flows of the project being evaluated.

Finally, and perhaps most important, is the assumption about a constant level of systematic risk. A company's WACC represents the overall return that the company earns, given the systematic risk of the existing collection of assets. It therefore follows that its WACC is applicable only to the evaluation of new investment opportunities that have a similar level of systematic risk.

It is this last requirement in particular that makes the WACC of Redskins particularly unsuitable for investment appraisal purposes, as it is a holding company consisting of a number of different subsidiaries in (presumably) different industries, and with the likelihood of different levels of systematic risk. Thus the WACC represents the required return on the average of these risks, but it cannot be thought to reflect the systematic risk of any one particular subsidiary.

Answer to problem 3

(a) The company is all-equity. Its cost of equity capital can be calculated either using the dividend valuation model or the capital asset pricing model.

Using CAPM: $E[r_{Bonzo}] = 11\% + (17\% - 11\%) \times 1.16$

$$= 17.96\% \text{ or } \underline{\underline{18\%}}$$

Using dividend valuation model:

$$d_0 = 5.99\text{p} \quad P_E = \frac{£13.35\text{m}}{30\text{m}} = \underline{44.5\text{p}}$$

g can be estimated either:
(i)   from past dividend growth rate

$$5.12(1 + g)^4 = 5.99$$

$$g = (5.99/5.12)^{1/4} - 1 = 0.04 \text{ or } \underline{4\%}$$

or

(ii) from $r \times b$ where

$$r = \frac{£0.0731 \times 30\text{m}}{£9.96\text{m}} = 0.22$$

$$b = \frac{7.31\text{p} - 5.99\text{p}}{7.31\text{p}} = 0.18$$

$$g = 0.22 \times 0.18 = 0.0396 \text{ or } \underline{4\%}$$

Hence $K_E = \dfrac{5.99(1 + 0.04)}{44.5} + 0.04 = 0.18 \text{ or } \underline{\underline{18\%}}$

NPV calculations:

Cement	−200	× 1	= −200	*Timber*	−150	× 1	= −150
Project	+100	× 0.8475	= + 84.75	*Project*	+ 75	× 0.8475	= + 63.56
	+100	× 0.7182	= + 71.82		+ 48.36	× 0.7182	= + 34.73
	+ 79.3	× 0.6086	= + 48.26		+ 75	× 0.6086	= + 45.64
		Accept	+ 4.83 NPV			*Reject*	− 6.07 NPV

(b) Bonzo's WACC reflects the company's *average* level of systematic risk. Hence it is unsuitable as a discount rate for projects in either division because it does not properly reflect the systematic risk involved, but only the company's average level. Instead, they should calculate specific risk-adjusted discount rates using CAPM:

$$E[r_{\text{Cement proj.}}] = 11\% + (17\% - 11\%) \times 1.50 = \underline{20\%}$$

$$E[r_{\text{Timber proj.}}] = 11\% + (17\% - 11\%) \times 0.50 = \underline{14\%}$$

Revised NPV calculations:

Cement	−200	× 1	= −200	*Timber*	−150	× 1	= −150
proj.	+100	× 0.8333	= + 83.33	*proj.*	+ 75	× 0.8772	= + 65.79
[20%]	+100	× 0.6944	= + 69.44	[14%]	+ 48.36	× 0.7695	= + 37.21
	+ 79.3	× 0.5787	= + 45.89		+ 75	× 0.6750	= + 50.62
		Reject	− 1.34 NPV			*Accept*	+ 3.62 NPV

(c) Referring to Fig. 13.1 if Bonzo uses WACC to evaluate its projects, it runs the risk of applying too low a discount rate to the high-risk projects of the cement division and too high a discount rate to the low-risk projects of the timber division. Therefore it may find itself (as in this question) accepting projects which it should be rejecting and vice versa.

By using CAPM, the company can generate discount rates for individual projects (or divisions) which reflect the systematic risk involved.

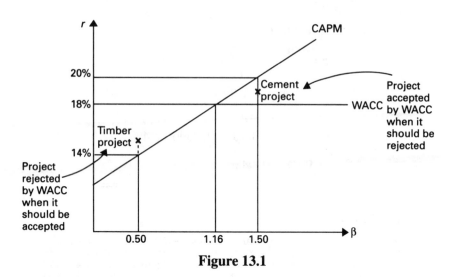

Figure 13.1

Answer to problem 4

(a) (i)   The dividend valuation model is:

$$K_E = \frac{d_0(1 + g)}{P_E} + g$$

The total dividend payout is given as £2.14m and the number of shares in issue is 10m. Thus the dividend per share, d_0, is £2.14m ÷ 10m = 21.4p.

The market price per share, P_E, is given as 321p (assumed to be ex div.) and the dividend growth rate, g, is given as 11%. Therefore:

$$K_E = \frac{21.4(1 + 0.11)}{321} + 0.11 = 0.184 \text{ or } \underline{18.4\%}$$

The company's cost of equity capital is 18.4%.

As the company's debt capital can be assumed, from the question, to be risk-free, then $K_D = r_F = 12\%$ (the Treasury Bill yield or return on government stock).

Therefore K_D after tax is: 12% (1 − 0.35) = $\underline{7.8\%}$

Given the company's gearing ratio of 1:2, the WACC is:

$$K_0 = 18.4\% \times \frac{2}{3} + 7.8\% \times \frac{1}{3} = \underline{14.87\%}$$

(ii)   The CAPM is:

$$E[r_{company}] = r_F + (E[r_M] - r_F)\, \beta_{company}$$

The company's beta for its equity is not given so has to be calculated from first principles using the beta equation:

$$\beta_{company} = \frac{\sigma_{company} \times \rho_{company, \ market}}{\sigma_{market}}$$

The question gives:

$$\sigma_{company} = 20\%$$
$$\sigma_{market \ portfolio} = 10\%$$
$$\rho_{company, \ market} = +0.7$$

Therefore $\beta_{company} = \dfrac{20\% \times 0.7}{10\%} = \dfrac{14\%}{10\%} = \underline{1.40}$

Also, given that the risk-free return (r_F) is 12% and the return on the market portfolio $E(r_M)$ is 16% , then the CAPM can be used to find the company's cost of equity capital $E[r_{company}]$:

$$E[r_{company}] = 12\% + [16\% - 12\%] \times 1.40 = \underline{17.6\%}$$

As before, the after-tax cost of debt capital is 7.8% and so the WACC is:

$$K_0 = 17.6\% \times \frac{2}{3} + 7.8\% \times \frac{1}{3} = 14.33\%$$

Assumptions made
(i)   The quoted share price is ex div.
(ii)   The share price represents an equilibrium value in an efficient market.
(iii)   The dividend growth rate is expected to remain constant in perpetuity.
(iv)   The company can obtain tax relief on the debt capital.
(v)   The values used for r_F and $E[r_M]$ are both appropriate, given the fact that the calculations are being carried out in a taxed world (i.e. we assume that they are both after-tax values).

Generally speaking, we would *not* expect these two share valuation models to give very similar estimates for the company's cost of equity capital because:
(i)   this version of the dividend growth model assumes, unrealistically, constant dividend growth in perpetuity;
(ii)   the dividend valuation model produces a multi-time period rate of return whilst the CAPM produces a single-time period rate of return.

If the assumption on dividend growth is valid and if the values for r_F and $E[r_M]$ are expected to remain approximately constant in the foreseeable future, then the two models may well produce similar results for the estimation of K_E, and so, K_0.

(b)   Four main practical problems can be specified.

    (i)   Should the management be using such a model to generate NPV discount rates? The CAPM is a single-period model and so produces a single period's required rate of return. It is not legitimate to then use this in a multi-period analysis like NPV, unless it can be assumed that r_F and $E[r_M]$ will remain constant over the life of the project.

    (ii)   How should the management go about estimating the project beta? Usually, the industry beta is taken as a surrogate, but there are many problems to this approach. The project may be *atypical* (i.e. not reflecting the average) of the industry. The industry group may not be homogeneous and so the industry beta simply reflects an average of the different parts of the industry group. There may not be an industry group beta available.

    (iii)   How should management go about identifying r_F and $E[r_M]$? With r_F what is required is an after-tax risk-free return. The tax rate used should be the personal tax rate of the marginal investor – a figure which is difficult to find in practice. The return on government stock (Treasury Bills) which is usually used is only risk-free in *money* terms, not in purchasing power terms. Usually, the excess market return, $E[r_M] - r_F$, is estimated. Again, there is the problem of making the correct adjustment for tax. Also, the excess market return tends to be relatively volatile and so a longer-run average has to be used. But over what time period should the average be calculated? Different time period averages give significantly different values.

    (iv)   Finally, the CAPM only reflects a project's systematic risk. The management within a company hold undiversified work portfolios and so they, personally, will be concerned with the project's total risk. Thus the management may feel that they require a higher expected return from a project than that indicated by the CAPM, as a reward for the *unsystematic* risk that it brings to the firm.

14

The capital structure decision in a no-tax world

Answer to problem 1

		Alpha		Beta	
(a)	Earnings	£	5.0m	£	5.0m
	Interest	£	0.72m		–
	Dividends	£	4.28m	£	5.0m
	P_E		100p		50p
	P_D	£	50		–
	V_E	£	17.2m	£	23.2m
	K_E		0.249		0.216
	K_D		0.18		–
	K_0		0.236		0.216

β shareholding: 464,000 shares = 1%

∴ Annual divs. = £50,000

Arbitrage to α: Sell β for £232,000, and either

α geared 4:17.2
∴ Buy £ 43,774 debt × 0.18   = £ 7,879 interest
      £188,226 equity × 0.249 = £46,838 dividends
                               £54,717 income

∴ £4,717/year better off

or

Buy 1% α debt, plus the balance in equity:

£40,000 debt	× 0.18	= £ 7,200	interest
£192,000 equity	× 0.249	= £47,808	dividends
		£55,008	income

∴ £5,008/year better off

As a shareholder in Beta, Ms Gamma holds no financial risk as Beta is an all-equity company. In order to be able to compare like with like it is necessary for her to maintain this zero exposure to financial risk when she moves into Alpha. Thus she wishes to buy into the *earnings* probability distribution of Alpha (which, by definition, has the same degree of business risk as Beta's *dividend* distribution). The simplest way would be to buy debt and equity in Alpha in proportion to the company's existing gearing ratio. However, this is not a perfect answer as Alpha's equity – and hence the gearing ratio – is in disequilibrium. Therefore the alternative arbitraging mechanism that is shown above may be preferred, as it effectively has Ms Gamma buying into Alpha in proportion to the equilibrium gearing ratio.

(b)   In equilibrium, given that the earnings of the two companies have the same magnitude:

$$V_{0\alpha} = V_{0\beta} = V_{e\beta} \qquad = \text{£23.2m}$$
$$V_{D\alpha} \qquad\qquad\qquad = \text{£ 4.0m}$$
$$\therefore V_{E\alpha} \qquad\qquad\qquad \underline{\text{£19.2m}}$$

$$P_{E\alpha} = \text{£19.2m}/17.2\text{m} = \text{£1.12/share}$$

Answer to problem 2

(a)   If two companies are in the same business risk class then their asset betas will be the same. Given that these two companies are in the same business risk class, this condition should hold. Furthermore, as Chardonnay is all-equity, its equity beta will equal its asset beta. Hence its equity beta can be estimated as Cabernet's asset beta:

β Cabernet assets = $1.6 \times 3/4 = 1.2 = $ β Chardonnay equity

(b)   *Cabernet*

$$K_E = 10\% + (6\% \times 1.6) = 19.6\%$$
$$K_D \qquad\qquad\qquad\qquad = 10\ \%$$
$$K_0 = (19.6\% \times 0.75) + (10\% \times 0.25) = 17.2\%$$

Chardonnay

$$K_E = 10\% + (6\% \times 1.2) = 17.2\% = K_0$$

This is just the result that the Modigliani and Miller no-tax capital structure hypothesis would expect: companies in the same business risk class have the same weighted average costs of capital.

(c)   Given the information in (b) above, a regular £150 per year dividend should have a value of £150/0.172 = £872.09. Thus the shareholder is, in effect, being offered a disequilibrium price for his shares. This price implies a WACC of: £150/£1,000 = 15%. Hence there would be a gain to be made by arbitraging into Cabernet. This can be achieved as follows.
   (i)   Sell shares in Chardonnay for £1,000 cash.
   (ii) Use the money to buy both the debt and equity of Cabernet in the same proportion as Cabernet's own debt: equity ratio (1:3). Thus the investor should purchase £250 of Cabernet debt and £750 of Cabernet equity. This would have the effect of maintaining a zero financial risk level (as at present) and would produce an annual income of:

$$£250 \times 0.10 \ = £\ 25$$
$$£750 \times 0.196 = \underline{£147}$$
$$£172/\text{year}$$

Thus the investor is £172 − £150 = £22/year better off, with no change in risk.

(d)   In these circumstances, Cabernet's WACC value of 17.2% is an equilibrium value. Hence Chardonnay's WACC (and hence K_E also, as it is an all-equity company) should equal 17.2%. Thus the equilibrium value of the investor's shareholding in Chardonnay is £150/0.172 = £872.09.

Answer to problem 3

(a)   Given the assumptions specified in the question and the conclusion of the Modigliani and Miller capital structure hypothesis in a no-tax environment, we would expect both companies to have the same WACC. As the shares of the all-equity company are in equilibrium then Geer Ltd's WACC should equal Ekwitty Ltd's cost of equity capital. See Fig. 14.1. As this is not the case, and that as Geer Ltd's WACC is above its predicted value we can conclude that the ordinary shares of Geer Ltd are currently undervalued (i.e. the disequilibrium market value of £400,000 is below the equilibrium value).

Geer Ltd   *Ekwitty Ltd*

$$K_D = \frac{80,000}{1,000,000} = \underline{0.08}$$

$$K_E = \frac{100,000}{400,000} = \underline{0.25} \qquad K_E = \frac{180,000}{1,800,000} = \underline{0.10}$$

$$K_0 = \frac{180,000}{1,400,000} = \underline{0.1286} \qquad K_0 = \frac{180,000}{1,800,000} = \underline{0.10}$$

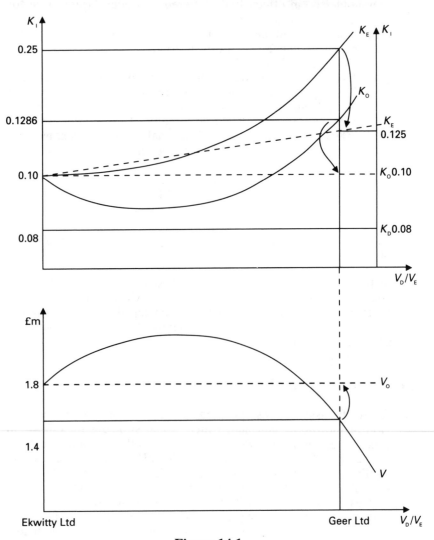

Figure 14.1

(b) See Fig. 14.1
(c) As the shares in Geer Ltd are undervalued, there are arbitrage gains to be made by a holder of shares in Ekwitty Ltd switching to Geer Ltd. The switch can be made and a zero financial risk level held constant, by an investor selling his shares in Ekwitty and buying both debt and equity in Geer Ltd in the same proportions as Geer's gearing ratio. Thus, if an individual has £1,000 of shares in Ekwitty Ltd:

Sell shares in Ekwitty Ltd: £1,000

As Geer Ltd has a debt equity ratio of 10:4, the following securities in Geer are purchased (rounded to whole pounds): £714 of debt capital and £286 of equity capital.

Annual dividend from Ekwitty Ltd: £1000 × 0.10 = <u>£100</u>
Annual interest from Geer Ltd: £ 714 × 0.08 = £ 57.12
Annual dividend from Geer Ltd: £ 286 × 0.25 = £ 71.50
Total annual income from Geer Ltd = £128.62

Therefore the arbitrager gains <u>£28.62</u> per year as a result, with no change in either business or financial risk.

15
Capital structure in a world with tax

Answer to problem 1

(a) *Mandina plc*

Using the asset beta, the CAPM can be used to calculate what would be the company's cost of capital, if it were all-equity financed:

$$7\% + (15\% - 7\%) \times 0.50 = \underline{11\%}$$

Hence Mandina, if it were all-equity financed, would have a value of:

$$\frac{£500,000(1 - 0.35)}{0.11} = \underline{£2.954\text{m}}$$

Using the Modigiani and Miller (M and M) expression for the total market value of a geared company in a taxed world, the actual total market value of Mandina can be estimated:

Total market value: £2.954m + (£1m × 0.35) = $\underline{£3.304\text{m}}$

As Mandina's debt is worth £1m, its equity will be worth: £3.304m – £1m = $\underline{£2.304\text{m}}$. As there is an 8% chance of bankruptcy and a cost of bankruptcy of £0.5m, the expected cost of bankruptcy will be: £0.5m × 0.08 = £40,000.

Therefore:

Total market value of equity	= $\underline{£2.304\text{m}}$
Total market value of debt	= $\underline{£1\text{m}}$
Total market value of company	= $\underline{£3.304\text{m}}$
Debt:equity ratio	= $\underline{1:2.234}$

Clarice plc

Company's cost of capital, assuming all-equity financing:

$$7\% + (15\% - 7\%) \times 1.50 = \underline{\underline{19\%}}$$

Value of company if all-equity financed:

$$\frac{£1.2m(1 - 0.35)}{0.19} = \underline{\underline{£4.105m}}$$

Total market value of company: $£4.105m + £1m \times 0.35 = \underline{\underline{£4.455m}}$

Total market value of company:	£4.455m
Less: total market value debt:	£1.000m
Total market value equity:	£3.455m

Less expected cost of bankruptcy: $10\% \times £0.5m = \underline{\underline{£50,000}}$

Total market value of equity:	£3.405m
Total market value of debt:	£1m
Total market value of company:	£4.405m
Debt:equity ratio	= 1:3.405

(b) There are, perhaps, four principal determinants behind the capital structure decision in practice:
  (i)   bankruptcy costs;
  (ii) agency costs;
  (iii) debt capacity;
  (iv) tax exhaustion.
Each of these will be discussed in turn to examine how they affect the capital structure decision.

Debt finance involves firms in a contractual agreement to pay interest and repay the capital sum. If the firm defaults on the agreement, debt holders can appoint receivers and effectively bankrupt the firm. Except in the case of fraud, firms are only going to default on loan agreements when there is insufficient cash flow. Thus, the more highly geared the company, the greater the chance of a shortfall in cash flow and hence the greater the chance of bankruptcy.

Although shareholders (and others, such as employees) no doubt bear a cost in such circumstances – as the question illustrates – the actual cost of bankruptcy is likely to represent only a very small loss in the wealth of a shareholder who has a well-diversified portfolio. However, in contrast, a very substantial loss would be suffered by the company directors in such circumstances – loss of office and loss of confidence in their professional abilities –

and this would particularly be the case for the finance director whose responsibility it is for the company's gearing level.

Thus directors are going to be cautious about the level of corporate gearing so as to keep the probability of bankruptcy – and the associated costs that they would bear – at an acceptably low level. Whether this results in low gearing or higher gearing depends not only upon the risk attitudes of the directors concerned, but also on the volatility of the company's pre-interest cash flow. Thus the directors of a property company, with its very stable (rental income) cash flow, may well be willing to gear the company up to high levels because even then the probability of loan default and consequent bankruptcy is relatively low. On the other hand, an engineering company's directors may only indulge in a low level of gearing because of that type of company's much more volatile cash flow.

The second factor is agency costs. When a company raises debt capital, the loan is made under a trust deed which has attached to it a series of restrictive conditions. These conditions represent part of the lender's efforts to control the actions of the management to ensure that they act responsibly with the money lent. In essence, these conditions represent 'agency costs'.

Generally speaking, the more highly geared the company, the more restrictive become these conditions. (Restrictions may be placed on such things as dividend growth, asset sales, diversification and further increases in gearing). Thus once again management may wish to restrict the level of gearing simply to avoid the more onerous of these agency costs being imposed.

The third factor is concerned with the fact that most corporate lending is secured against the assets of the firm. However, different assets have different levels of ability to act as security for a loan. This is referred to as an asset's debt capacity. The main determinants of debt capacity are, firstly, the efficiency/quality of the second-hand market and, secondly, the rate of depreciation. The greater the former and the slower the latter, the better will be an asset's ability to act as security. Thus, property assets will have a high debt capacity and industrial machinery will have a low debt capacity.

Therefore the directors' choice as to the company's gearing level may well be dictated by the debt capacity of the firm's assets and hence the capital market's willingness to supply debt capital. Returning to the example used earlier, even if an engineering company's directors were willing to ignore bankruptcy costs, it is likely that they would be prevented from gearing the firm up to high levels by the low debt capacity. However, the capital markets would be willing to gear up the property company's capital structure because of its high debt capacity.

The final determinant of the gearing ratio arises from the fact that the main attraction of debt capital is the tax-deductibility of the interest payments. Tax exhaustion refers to the situation where the firm has insufficient tax liability to take the tax relief available. In such circumstances, much of the attractiveness of debt, relative to equity, disappears. Thus companies may well restrict their level of gearing to avoid the possibility of moving into a situation of tax exhaustion.

Finally, no mention has been made in this discussion of the weighted average cost of capital (WACC). The reason for this is that firstly most companies are unable to measure their WACC with any confidence (principally because of valuation difficulties), and even when they do, the WACC is such a volatile figure that company directors cannot realistically indulge in the static analysis of the 'traditional view' of capital structure, seeking to identify the minimum point on the WACC function. Certainly companies might try to identify some 'optimal' capital structure, but its optimality is more likely to be based on managerial judgement arising out of the four factors discussed earlier, rather than on an estimate of the WACC function.

Also, mention should also be made of the M and M analysis. M and M suggested that, in a taxed world, companies should gear up as high as possible in order to take advantage of debt interest tax relief. Implicit in the foregoing discussion is the assumption that this is the policy that directors would wish to pursue, but they are prevented from always following this advice because of the factors discussed.

In addition, the later Miller analysis (1977) throws all this analysis into some confusion. Miller argued that in a world of corporate and personal taxes and a perfect market for corporate debt capital, the capital structure decision (from an M and M viewpoint) is irrelevant. However such circumstances – if they hold good in the real world – still do not negate the impact of the four factors discussed on the capital structure decision.

Answer to problem 2

(a) (i) The cost of equity using the dividend growth model

$$K_E = \frac{d_0(1+g)}{V_E} + g$$

$$\text{Company A} = \frac{4.3(1.12)}{164} + 0.12 = 14.9\%$$

$$\text{Company B} = \frac{8.2(1.1)}{280} + 0.10 = 13.2\%$$

$$\text{Company C} = \frac{2.4(1.19)}{303} + 0.19 = 19.9\%$$

$$\text{Company D} = \frac{9.9(1.22)}{470} + 0.22 = 24.6\%$$

(ii)   The cost of equity using the CAPM

$$K_E = r_f + (E[r_m] - r_f)\beta$$

Company A $= 11 + (9 \times 0.75) = 17.8\%$

Company B $= 11 + (9 \times 0.88) = 18.9\%$

Company C $= 11 + (9 \times 1.24) = 22.2\%$

Company D $= 11 + (9 \times 1.26) = 22.3\%$

The two models give significantly different results particularly for Company B, making a reliable estimate of K_E difficult to achieve. The differences may be attributable to a number of factors but the most important may be that both estimates use past data to estimate K_E. The cost of equity is the rate of return that existing and potential shareholders require in order to persuade them to invest in the company. Therefore it is concerned with expectations for the future, future returns and future interest rates. Both models used above base the estimate of K_E on past data. The dividend model uses past growth as a estimate of future growth. The beta values used in the CAPM calculations are presumably calculated from observations of past share price movements (i.e. the slope of the regression line of r_j on r_m). In the subsequent calculations K_E has been taken as an approximate mid-point between the two estimates given above. The resultant WACCs are obviously very approximate.

(iii)   Calculation of the weighted average cost of capital (K_0)

K_0 is usually calculated as $K_0 = \dfrac{K_E V_E + K_D V_D}{V_E + V_D}$. However all four companies are virtually all equity (the most highly geared, Company A, has less than 1% debt). The following calculations are included for the sake of completeness although given the crude estimates of K_E the resultant 'accuracy' is entirely spurious.

Note $K_D = 12(1 - 0.45) = 6.6\%$

Company A $\dfrac{(0.16 \times 68) + (0.066 \times 0.6)}{68 + 0.6}$ $= 15.9\%$

Company B $\dfrac{(0.16 \times 63.2) + (0.066 \times 0.1)}{63.2 + 0.1}$ $= 16.0\%$

Company C   ungeared $\therefore K_0 = K_E$ $= 21\%$

$$\text{Company D} \quad \frac{(0.23 \times 123.4) + (0.066 \times 0.3)}{123.4 + 0.3} = 23\%$$

(b) As all four companies are virtually entirely financed by equity capital, the differences in K_0 are due to differences in K_E. In discussing why the K_Es are different, the first point to be made is that they may not be! As was noted in the answer to part (a) above, both models produce estimates which may or may not be reliable. Generally speaking, both the dividend valuation model and the CAPM are more likely to produce reliable results for a sample of comparable risk firms from a given risk class than for an individual company. Furthermore, the constant growth model is likely to be particularly unreliable for companies with unstable or high growth rates (e.g. C and D).

Accepting these points, it is clear that the estimates of K_E do not significantly differ for either A and B or C and D especially if the estimate is based on the CAPM, which should prove to be the more reliable model. (In a survey of the individual beta values of utilities companies in the USA, Brealey and Myers show that the standard error is approximately one-third of the estimated beta value.)

While there may not be significant differences between A and B or C and D there is a marked difference between the groupings of A, B and C, D. To understand the possible reasons for this it is first necessary to appreciate that the capitalization rate is largely a function of the risks associated with the various companies. Since all four companies have very low gearing ratios, financial risk will be relatively insignificant and the differences in the rates must be attributable to differences in the business or operating risks of the companies. The market clearly sees electronics as a more risky investment than brewing and the management of public houses.

It may also be worth noting that while all of the companies have very little long-term debt, Company B does have a substantial bank overdraft. Strictly, this is repayable on demand and may raise questions about B's liquidity position. In turn this may go some way to explaining the fact that B's beta value is higher than A's.

Finally, the ratio of market value to book value is much higher for C and D than for A and B, i.e. the present value of the earnings stream is much greater than the book value of the assets. The lack of a substantial asset basis for the total values of C and D may be seen as contributing to the higher risks associated with C and D and hence to their higher beta values and K_Es.

(c) The M and M with-tax analysis shows that:

$$V_{0_g} = V_{E_{ug}} + V_D T_c$$

For financial managers the significance of this result is that the value of the business can always be increased by substituting debt for equity and therefore the optimal capital structure is 99.9% debt.

It is clear that this conclusion has not influenced the managers of companies A, B, C and D. Furthermore it is also clear that it has not influenced many managers in practice. Companies with 99.9% debt are fairly thin on the ground. The reasons for the reluctance of financial managers to take M and M's conclusions literally may be found by considering two factors not included in M and M's model. These are the effects of personal taxation and the costs of bankruptcy and financial distress.

In essence, M and M argue that the value of a geared company is its value as an ungeared company, plus a premium which is the present value of the tax shield resulting from the fact that loan interest is an allowable expense for corporation tax purposes. In practice, the magnitude of the present value of the tax shield may be reduced, if not eliminated, by two factors. The first is that loan interest payments only offer tax reliefs to companies with corporation tax liabilities. In recent years in the UK the combination of a recession, high initial capital allowances for new investment and stock appreciation relief has meant that the effective rate of corporation tax (and hence the potential for tax relief) has been much lower than the nominal rate. Many companies may have exhausted their tax liabilities well before they attained the high gearing levels implied by the M and M model.

Secondly, M and M base their conclusions on the fact that it is more corporation-tax efficient to pay returns to investors in the form of returns to debt rather than returns to equity. However, if the total tax bill on corporate earnings is considered (i.e. corporate and personal taxes paid by investors), the conclusions may differ. Paradoxically, it was Merton Miller (of M and M fame) who suggested that the introduction of personal taxes into the model might change the conclusions. While it may be corporation-tax efficient to pay interest rather than returns to equity, there are personal tax advantages in receiving returns to equity rather than debt. The first is that dividends carry with them a tax credit and no further personal tax is payable by basic-rate tax payers. Secondly, it is possible to pay at least part of the return to equity in the form of capital gains rather than dividend or interest and these are taxed less onerously than other forms of income.

These personal tax advantages will have no relevance to investors, such as pension funds, that do not pay income tax. Hence, according to Miller, it should be possible to 'bribe' a category of investors with a higher rate and persuade them to accept debt rather than equity. Initially, the cost of the bribe can be met from the corporation tax savings, resulting in a net gain to the company. However as these zero and low personal tax investors are satisfied it will become increasingly difficult to reap a net advantage from gearing up. The personal tax disadvantages will offset the corporation tax advantages. The important point to note is that the low personal tax payers represent an aggregate potential investment in debt, i.e. for the market as a whole. In a stable market (i.e. in equilibrium) these investors will hold all the debt they wish to hold and it will not be possible for an individual company to make any further gains by increasing gearing.

The second broad category of factors not considered in the M and M model are the costs of bankruptcy and financial distress. M and M do not ignore the possibility of bankruptcy but they do consider it to be a costless exercise. In practice there are two real costs. Firstly the professional and legal costs of bankruptcy and secondly the costs resulting from selling assets below their worth in a forced sale situation. Brealey and Myers suggest there are other costs, short of bankruptcy, resulting from high gearing. These are the 'costs of financial distress and include such things as losses resulting from restrictions on management imposed by debenture trustees, loss of revenues resulting from lack of customer confidence, costs resulting from the reluctance of suppliers to give normal credit terms and the loss of high calibre staff fearing redundancy in the event of bankruptcy. Brealey and Myers argue that the value of the geared company is the value of the ungeared company plus the present value of the tax shield less the expected present value of the costs of financial distress (including the costs of bankruptcy). As gearing increases, the danger of bankruptcy increases and so does the expected value of the cost of financial distress. The maximum value of the firm may well be obtained well short of 99.9% debt.

In conclusion, it may well be the case that a company's capital structure may affect its total value but in a mature market it may not be possible for financial managers to act positively to increase value by manipulating the gearing ratio. This is because it is aggregate gearing in the market as a whole that is relevant rather than the gearing of individual companies. In fact, from a managerial decision making view-point, it may well be that M and M's original conclusion in their 1957 'no-tax' hypothesis is the most relevant, i.e. managers cannot influence corporate values through their financing decisions. Of course this is at variance with both the traditional view and M and M's with-tax hypothesis. A reasonable compromise may be found between the two positions. Borrowing may make sense for some firms but not for others, depending on the likelihood of gaining an advantage from the tax shield. This in turn depends on whether or not the firm expects to have taxable profits. If it does, there is likely to be a net advantage from borrowing. If it does not, there will be a net disadvantage.

Answer to problem 3

Modigliani and Miller show that companies which have the same earnings stream and the same level of business risk will have the same total market values (V_0) in the absence of taxation, whatever their individual capital structures. Dora and Bella are two such companies and so it is not surprising that in t_{-3}, when there was no taxation in Despina, their total market values were identical:

$$\text{Dora: } V_E = V_0 = \$1m$$
$$\text{Bella: } V_E + V_D = V_0 = \$0.8m + \$0.2m = \$1m$$

In the following year taxation was introduced on company profits and therefore company market values could be expected to fall. However, under the t_{-2} regime there was no difference between the tax treatment of equity dividends and debt interest. Therefore the tax charge was unaffected by a company's capital structure. Consequently, the total market values of the two companies should remain the same, despite their different gearing ratios. This was the case:

$$\text{Dora: } V_E = V_0 = \$0.51m$$
$$\text{Bella: } V_E + V_D = V_0 = \$0.51m$$

In t_{-1} the tax regime was changed so that debt interest was treated differently from equity dividends. Specifically, debt interest was now allowable against taxation. Thus a geared company would have a lower tax charge than a similar ungeared company and, as a result, the geared company would have a higher total market value.

Again Modigliani and Miller showed that under such a tax regime with two identical companies, except that one was geared while the other was ungeared, then the total market value of the geared company would be:

$$V_0 \text{ (geared)} = V_0 \text{ (ungeared)} + V_D \cdot T_c$$

where T_c is the rate of corporation tax. Therefore it would be expected that Bella (the geared company) would have a greater market value than Dora:

$$\text{Dora: } V_E = V_0 = \$0.52m$$
$$\text{Bella: } V_E + V_D = V_0 + \$0.60m$$

and this value for Bella can be shown to fit in with the M and M expression:

$$V_0 \text{ (Bella)} = V_0 \text{ (Dora)} + (V_D \text{ (Bella)} \times T_C)$$
$$\$0.6m \quad = \$0.52m + (\$0.16m \times 0.50)$$

Finally, in t_0, although the tax regime remained unchanged from t_{-1}, there is effectively no corporation tax as tax allowances shield operating earnings fully.

Therefore, once again, the total market values of the two companies would be expected to equate, as they do:

$$\text{Dora: } V_E = V_0 = \$0.98\text{m}$$
$$\text{Bella: } V_E + V_D = V_0 = \$0.98\text{m}$$

16
The capital structure decision in practice

Answer to problem 1

Calculations

Current EPS

$$\frac{£5.778m}{10m} = 57.78p$$

Current gearing (debt/equity using book values)

$$\frac{£12m + £6m}{£22.02m} = 81.7\%$$

Impact on EPS and gearing of the three different sources of finance

This question gives no indication as to the impact on earnings of the extra £10m of investment. Thus it will be assumed that it will generate the same return on investment as at present.

$$\text{Operating profit:} \quad \frac{£11.17m}{£34.02m} = 32.8\%$$
$$\text{Capital employed:}$$

Thus the extra £10m of capital will generate extra operating profits of:

$$£10m \times 0.328 = \underline{£3.28m}$$

In addition, it will be assumed that the company will maintain its current dividend per share payout.

(i) *Ordinary share financing*
It is assumed that the new shares will be issued at a 10% discount on the current share price of 350p: 315p.

Thus, the number of new shares issued will be:

$$£10m/315p = 3,175,000 \text{ approx.}$$

Also, it is assumed that the company will maintain its current dividend per share payout of:

$$\frac{£3.467m}{10m} = 34.67p/share$$

		£m
Operating profit	11.17 + 3.28 =	14.45
Interest		2.28
Pre-tax profit		12.17
Tax at 35%		4.26
Earnings		7.91
Dividends	(10m + 3.175m) × 34.67p =	4.57
Retained earnings		3.34

Revised EPS: $\dfrac{£7.91m}{13.175m} = \underline{60p}$

Revised gearing: $\dfrac{£12m + £6m}{£22.02m + £10m + £3.34m} = \underline{50.9\%}$

(ii) *Preference share financing*

	£m
Operating profit	14.45
Interest	2.28
Pre-tax profit	12.17
Tax at 35%	4.26
Earnings	7.91
Preference dividends	1.40
Earnings available for shareholders	6.51
Dividends	3.467
Retained earnings	3.043

Revised EPS: $\dfrac{£6.51m}{10m} = \underline{65.1p}$

Revised gearing: $\dfrac{£12m + £6m + £10m}{£22.02m + £3.043m} = \underline{111.7\%}$

(iii)   *Loan stock financing*

	£m
Operating profit	14.45
Interest 2.28 + 1.2	3.48
Pre-tax profit	10.97
Tax at 35%	3.84
Earnings	7.13
Dividend	3.467
Retained earnings	3.663

Revised EPS: $\dfrac{£7.13m}{10m} = \underline{71.3p}$

Revised gearing: $\dfrac{£12m + £6m + £10m}{£22.02m + £3.663m} = \underline{109\%}$

Report to the Directors of Latost plc

Dear Sirs,

We have analysed the probable impact of the three proposed financing packages of the company's EPS and gearing levels. The results are shown below:

	EPS	*Gearing*
Current situation	57.78p	81.7%
Equity financing	60p	50.9%
Preference financing	65.1p	111.7%
Loan stock financing	71.3p	109%

All three financing packages will result in an increase in EPS. Financing via preference shares or loan stock will increase the level of gearing, while financing with equity will reduce the gearing.

The decision as to what financing package should be chosen is not clear-cut. However, the analysis would appear to suggest that loan stock financing is a better alternative to preference share financing as the loan stock alternative provides a significantly higher EPS and a marginally lower level of gearing.

This then narrows the choice between equity financing and loan stock financing. It is here that the directors must judge the trade-off that their shareholders will find acceptable between risk and return.

Equity financing results in a small increase in EPS from 57.78p to 60p, but does provide a substantial reduction in gearing (and hence, a reduction in the riskiness of ordinary shares) from 81.7% to 50.9%.

In contrast, loan stock financing results in a substantial increase in EPS from 57.78p to 71.3p, but it also increases the level of gearing from an already high 81.7% up to 109%.

We would suggest that the final choice be made after investigating the gearing levels of Latost's competitors. If the competitors have gearing levels of around 100%, then it would be reasonable to assume that such a high level of gearing is acceptable and, on balance, the loan stock option should be selected.

However, if Latost's competitors generally have a much lower level of gearing, then the equity financing alternative may represent the more acceptable course of action.

Yours faithfully,

B.E.R. Tie
Accountants

Answer to problem 2

(a) 'Business risk' arises out of the risky nature of the company's business, which manifests itself in the variability of the company's earnings stream (before interest and tax). Quite simply, some companies have very stable earnings streams because of the steady, low-risk nature of their businesses. A supermarket company might be one such example. In contrast, some other companies have highly volatile earnings, again because of the very variable high-risk nature of their businesses. A small oil-exploration company might serve as a suitable example of a company with a high degree of business risk.

Portfolio theory shows that risks can be divided up into systematic risk and unsystematic risk. Systematic risk is that part of total risk that cannot be diversified away; while unsystematic risk is the risk that can be diversified away. Therefore business risk is partially systematic and partially unsystematic.

The systematic element of business risk is largely (but not completely) out of the control of the individual company management. The unsystematic element of business risk arises out of factors which are specific to the individual company and are directly under the control of management.

The two main determinants of a company's exposure to systematic business risk would be the sensitivity of the company's revenues to the level of economic activity in the economy (and its sensitivity to macro-economic events in general), and its proportion of fixed-to-variable 'operating' costs, i.e. the costs incurred in generating those revenues – principally material, labour and energy costs. The greater its revenue sensitivity and the greater its proportion of fixed costs, the greater its exposure to systematic business risk.

Such factors as revenue sensitivity and fixed-to-variable operating costs are largely out of management's control, and arise out of the nature of the market and the production technology. Thus a carpet manufacturing business can do very little about the highly revenue-sensitive nature of the business (people buy new carpets when the economy booms and not otherwise). Nor can the manufacturer do much about the high proportion of fixed costs involved in carpet production technology.

However, it should be noted that these factors are not entirely out of management's control. For example, the carpet manufacturer may try to lock his customers into long-term deals to bring greater stability to the revenues. Similarly they may try to sub-contract out as much of the manufacturing process as they can, on short-term contracts, to keep as many of their costs variable as possible.

The unsystematic aspects of business risk arise from such factors as the skill of the top management team, the training of the work-force, the state of labour relations and the ability of the marketing department. Obviously, such factors are largely under the direct control of the management.

(b) An investor with a well-diversified share portfolio should have eliminated all unsystematic risk. Therefore such an investor is only going to be interested in the systematic element of business risk which, together with financial risk, goes to make up the beta value of the shares.

(c) (i) *Degree of operating gearing (DOG)*
DOG at a given level of turnover is:

$$\frac{\text{Turnover} - \text{variables costs}}{\text{Profit before interest and tax}}$$

At the start of the current financial year

$$\text{DOG} = \frac{3,381 - 2,193}{462} = 2.57$$

Assume that variable costs comprise wages and salaries, raw materials and direct selling expenses. (In reality these are not all likely to vary directly with turnover.)

One interpretation of a 2.57 DOG may be that a 1% change in sales will lead to a 2.57% change in profit before interest and tax (in the same direction).

At the end of the financial year, the expected profit and loss account, assuming no price changes except those stated, is:

	£000	£000
Turnover (15% increase)		3,888
Operating expenses:		
Wages and salaries (1,220 × 0.80 × 1.15)	1,122	
Raw materials (15% increase)	1,004	

Direct selling prices (15% increase)	115	
General administration (no increase)	346	
Other fixed costs (85% increase)	465	
		3,052
Profit before interest and tax		836

Therefore expected DOG at the end of the year is:

$$\frac{3,888 - 2,241}{836} = 1.97$$

The degree of operating gearing is expected to fall.

If a high percentage of a company's total costs are fixed, that company will have a high degree of operating gearing. If other factors are held constant the higher the operating gearing the higher will be the business risk of a company. In this case other factors *have not* been held constant; the unit variable cost of wages and salaries and also the level of fixed costs are expected to change. The overall result is a lower DOG at the sales level of £3,888,000.

Financial gearing
As an accounting-based analysis of the company is being undertaken, an accounting-based measure of financial gearing will be used:

$$\frac{\text{Balance sheet value of debt}}{\text{Shareholders funds}}$$

At the start of the year financial gearing is $\dfrac{570}{1,510} = 37.7\%$.

At the end of the year profit before interest and tax has been estimated to be £836,000.

	£000
Profit before interest and tax	836
Interest	207
Profit before tax	629
Tax	252
Profit available to ordinary shareholders	377
Estimated dividend	189
Retained earnings	188

Estimated financial gearing $\dfrac{570 + 820}{1,510 + 188} = 81.8\%$.

The expected financial gearing more than doubles by the end of the year. The higher the level of financial gearing, the higher the financial risk placed on the ordinary share-holders.

(ii) (1) If turnover increases by 15%, the expected profit available to ordinary shareholders is £377,000. There are 3,200,000 issued ordinary shares resulting in an expected earnings per share of 11.78 pence.

The earnings per share at the start of the year is

$$\frac{£227,000}{3,200,000} = 7.09 \text{ pence per share.}$$

Because of the financial and operating gearing effects, earnings per share are expected to increase by 66%.

(2) If turnover falls by 10%

	£000	£000
Turnover		3,043
Operating expenses:		
Wages and salaries (1,220 × 0.90 × 0.80)	878	
Raw materials (10% fall)	786	
Direct selling expenses (10% fall)	90	
General administration (no change)	346	
Other fixed costs (85% increase)	465	
		2,565
Profit before interest and tax		478
Interest		207
Profit before tax		271
Tax		108
Profit available to ordinary shareholders		163

The estimated earnings per share is $\dfrac{£163,000}{3,200,000}$

= 5.09 pence.

This is 28% lower than the current earnings per share.

The changes in the operating and financial gearing have increased the risks for the shareholders.

17
Investment and financing decision interactions

Answer to Problem 1

(a) *Base-case discount rate*

$$\beta_{\substack{\text{Asset} \\ \text{project}}} = \left[1.26 \times \frac{3}{3 + 1(1 - 0.35)} \right] + \left[0.10 \times \frac{1(1 - 0.35)}{3 + 1(1 - 0.35)} \right]$$

$$\beta_{\substack{\text{Asset} \\ \text{project}}} = 1.036 + 0.018 = \underline{1.054}$$

$$E[r_{\text{Project}}] = 7\% + [15.5\% - 7\%] \times 1.054 = 16\% \text{ approx.}$$

Base–case present value

$$-10,000 + 6,700\ (1 - 0.35)A_{\overline{3}|0.16} = \underline{-219\text{PV}}$$

Financing side-effects
PV tax shield

$$3,000 \times 0.14 \times 0.35\ A_{\overline{3}|0.14} = \underline{+341\ \text{PV}}$$

Issue costs

$$3,000 \times 0.01 \times (1 - 0.35) = -19.5$$

$$4,000 \times 0.02 \times (1 - 0.35) = \underline{-52}$$
$$-71.5\text{PV}$$

Note that the project gains the tax shield and incurs the issue costs based on how the project *would* be financed as a free–standing entity. Hence, assuming that £3,000 of retained earnings would be used and its 30% debt capacity would allow £3,000 of debt financing, this means that, under normal circumstances, £4,000 of equity finance (via a rights issue) would be raised.

Adjusted present value:

$-219 + 341 - 71.5 = \underline{+50.5 \text{ APV}}$ Accept.

(b) *Effect of cheap loan*

Interest saved: $10,000 \times 0.14 \times A_{\overline{3}|0.14}$ $= +3250$
Less lost tax shield: $10,000 \times 0.14 \times 0.35 A_{\overline{3}|0.14}$ $= \underline{-1138}$
                                                  $+2112$

Revised APV: $-219 + 2112 - 71.5 = \underline{+1821.5 \text{ APV}}$.

Note, as the cheap loan is *specifically* attached to this project, *all* of its net benefits are taken into account.

Answer to problem 2

(a) *Calculation of an asset beta for project*

$$\beta_{\text{Asset}} = \beta_{\text{Equity}} \times \frac{V_E}{V_E + V_D(1 - T_C)} + \beta_{\text{Debt}} \times \frac{V_D(1 - T_C)}{V_E + V_D(1 - T_C)}$$

$$\beta_{\text{Asset}} = 2.29 \times \frac{3}{3 + 2(1 - 0.35)} + 0.15 \times \frac{2(1 - 0.35)}{3 + 2(1 - 0.35)}$$

$$\beta_{\text{Asset}} = 1.60 + 0.04 = \underline{1.64}$$

Calculation of base-case discount rate for project

Base-case discount rate $= r_F + [E(r_M) - r_F] \times \beta_{\text{Asset}}$

$8.5\% + [15.5\% - 8.5\%] \times 1.64 = \underline{20\% \text{ approx}}$

Calculation of base-case present value for project

Data Capital expenditure: £1m
         Scrap value: £0.6m
         Working capital requirement: £0.3m
         Revenues: £1.1m/year for 5 years.
         Operating Expenses: Materials £0.25m/year.
                                Labour   £0.165m/year.
                                  Supervisory labour £0.056m/year.
                                  Training £0.270m at Year 1.
                                  Variable overheads £0.076m/year.
                                  Rent: £0.012m/year.
                                  Var. selling expenses: £0.095m/year.

[Note: Labour has been costed on an incremental basis. Depreciation has been excluded as it is a non-cash item. Financing cash flows – interest – have been excluded. All other non-incremental/allocated expenses have been excluded.]

Total operating expenses £0.654m/year
Net revenues £1.1m – £0.654m = £0.446m/year pre-tax.

Capital allowance tax relief

	Capital allowances			Tax relief	Year
£1m	× 0.25 = £0.25m	× 0.40 =	£0.1m	1
	0.25m				
£0.75m	× 0.25 = £0.1875m	× 0.40 =	£0.075m	2
	0.1875m				
£0.5625m	× 0.25 = £0.1406m	× 0.35 =	£0.0492m	3
	0.1406m				
£0.4219m	× 0.25 = £0.1055m	× 0.35 =	£0.0369m	4
	0.1055m				
£0.3164m	× 0.25 = £0.0791m	× 0.35 =	£0.0277m	5
	0.0791m				
£0.2373	– £0.6m = (£0.3627m)	× 0.35 =	(£0.1269m)	6

Cash flow analysis £m

	0	1	2	3	4	5	6
Machinery	(1)						
Scrap						0.6	
C.A. tax relief		0.1	0.075	0.0492	0.0369	0.0277	(0.1269)
W.C.	(0.3)					0.3	
Training		(0.270)					
Tax relief			0.108				
Net revenues		0.446	0.446	0.446	0.446	0.446	
Tax			(0.1784)	(0.1561)	(0.1561)	(0.1561)	(0.1561)
Net cash flow	(1.3)	0.276	0.4506	0.3391	0.3268	1.2176	(0.283)
20% Discount Rate		0.8333	0.6944	0.5787	0.4823	0.4019	0.3349
PV cash flow	(1.3)	0.23	0.3129	0.1962	0.1576	0.4893	(0.1061)

Base–case present value: (£20,100)

Calculation of present value of financing side effects

The debt capacity of the project is:

Capital expenditure: £1m × 0.50 = £0.5m
W.C. expenditure: £0.3m × 0.10 = £0.03m
Total £0.53m

Therefore the tax shield will only be calculated as a total of £530,000 of debt financing at 10% interest.

PV tax shield

$£530,000 \times 0.10 = £53,000$/year interest for 5 years.
$£\ 53,000 \times 0.40 = £21,200$ tax relief in Year 1.
$£\ 53,000 \times 0.35 = £18,550$ tax relief/year thereafter
PV: $£21,200\ (1 + 0.10)^{-2}$ $= £17,520$
$£18,550\ A_{\overline{4}|0.10}\ (1 + 0.10)^{-2} = £48,594$
$\underline{£66,114}$

Adjusted present value

Base-case present value $£\ (20,100)$
PV of tax shield $£\ \ \underline{66,114}$
APV + $£\ \ \underline{46,014}$

As the APV is positive, the project should be accepted.

(b) The evaluation carried out in part (a) differs in two fundamental
ways from the analysis carried out by the production director.
Firstly, the project was evaluated on the basis of incremental cash
flows. Therefore, a number of irrelevant items were excluded from
the analysis. Secondly, the project was evaluated on the basis of
APV and not NPV, to capture better the impact of the finance
package proposed for the project.

(c) Net present value is a capital expenditure evaluation technique. In
contrast, adjusted present value is able to evaluate not only the
capital expenditure decisions, but also the financing package with
which it is proposed to undertake the project. In this way, therefore,
APV is a more powerful form of analysis than the rather limited
NPV analysis.

Answer to problem 3

(a) Cash flows (£000s) associated with the loan (six–month time
periods)

	t_0	t_1	t_2	t_3	t_4	t_5	t_6	t_7
Loan	100							
Interest	(8)	(8)	(4)	(4)				
Tax relief				2.8		4.2		1.4
Repayments			(50)		(50)			
	92	(8)	(54)	(1.2)	(50)	4.2		1.4
6% Discount		0.9434	0.8900	0.8396	0.7921	0.7473	0.7050	0.6651
Factor	92	(7.547)	(48.06)	(1.007)	(39.605)	3.139	–	0.931

NPV is £149 which is approximately zero. Since the cash flows
associated with the loan have approximately a zero NPV when
discounted at 6% per year, the cash flows have an IRR of 6% per

year. Louise is correct in her calculation of the after-tax cost of debt.

(b) *PV of loan/purchase cash flows*

Year	WDA	Tax relief		Discount		PV	Timing
1	£23,000	£8,050	×	0.8396	=	£ 6759	t_3
2	£17,250	£6,040	×	0.7473	=	£ 4514	t_5
						£11,273	

Residual value at t_4 = £51,750
PV of residual value = £51,750 × 0.7921 = £40,991

PV of purchase cash flows

Cost of equipment	(92,000)
Tax relief	11,273
Residual value	40,991
PV loan/purchase cash flow	= (39,736)

PV lease cash flows

	t_0	t_1	t_2	t_3	t_4	t_5	t_6	t_7
Rental	(16)	(16)	(16)	(16)				
Tax relief				(5.6)		11.2		5.6
Net cash flow	(16)	(16)	(16)	(10.4)	–	11.2	–	5.6
6% Discount Factor		0.9434	0.8900	0.8396		0.7473		0.6651
PV cash flow	(16)	(15.094)	(14.24)	(8.732)	–	8.37	–	3.725

PV cost of leasing = (£41,971)

Since the present value cost of loan/purchase is less than the present value cost of leasing, the machine should be purchased with the help of the loan.

(c) Leases are contracts where one party, the lessee, hires capital equipment (or possibly a service) from another party, the lessor. Thus the lessor is the legal owner of the equipment, but the lessee uses or operates the equipment. Leases can be categorized roughly into either financial or operating leases.

Under a financial lease, the lessee agrees to make a series of payments to the lessor for the use of the equipment. The important distinguishing characteristics of such a lease is that the contract cannot be cancelled by either party during the operating life of the equipment. In contrast, operating leases are contracted, often for an unspecified period of time, but which is expected to be shorter than the life of the asset, and either side is allowed to cancel the contract at short notice. However, in practice, the distinction between financial and operating leases is not necessarily as clear–cut as this classification might suggest. Many leases represent a mixture of both types.

An alternative way of distinguishing between the two types of lease (and this may be more pertinent in respect of the present context) is that with a financial lease the lessor is assured of recovering the full cost of the equipment leased, together with a suitable return on capital. Hence the risks of using the asset are held entirely by the lessee. On the other hand, with an operating lease, the lessor would not necessarily expect to recover the full capital cost of the equipment (plus return) out of the lease payments, but would also take into account the future recovery of the asset and its subsequent second–hand value. Therefore with this latter type of lease the risks of ownership remain largely with the lessor rather than the lessee.

A financial lease will normally involve a contract that is similar to that of any other type of secured loan agreement in that it will usually contain covenants that require a minimum level of liquidity to be maintained and/or a maximum gearing ratio. Thus a financial lease can be viewed simply as a form of debt instrument or debt financing which effectively secures the services (but not the legal ownership) of an asset.

However, it is sometimes held that because such an asset is not legally the property of the lessee and therefore does not appear in the balance sheet, the lease payments should not or need not be considered as a liability which affects a company's gearing ratio. Such a view is erroneous because any potential lender of finance to a company is bound to take contractual financial lease obligations into account in a similar way as with ordinary debt finance. Nor can it be claimed that the covenants attached to a financial lease are likely to be any less onerous than those attached to normal debt financing.

Therefore the only advantage of a financial lease over (say) issuing debt capital to buy the equipment outright arises from tax considerations. In particular, a company which finds itself in either a temporary or a permanent non-tax paying position may find it advantageous to lease, as the lessor is able to acquire ownership of the asset, obtain the tax relief that is available and then pass (some) of this on to the lessee in the form of lower lease payments.

With operating leases, the main advantage for the lessee is the option of cancellation at short notice. Gaining the use of an asset via an operating lease means that the lessee does not bear the risk of obsolescence or the risk of being the owner of an unwanted asset, caused by a reduction in demand for that asset's output. Given this lack of commitment from the lessee's point of view, an operating lease has significantly less financial consideration than a financing lease. Hence, unlike a financial lease, it is unlikely that an operating lease would be included in any consideration of a firm's gearing ratio. Furthermore, operating lease payments are likely to be included as part of the general operating costs of a machine in an investment appraisal. Financing lease costs are likely to be considered separately in a specific financing evaluation.

In addition, because of the cancellation option (and therefore with the full risks of ownership being borne by the lessor), the explicit cost of an operating lease is likely to be greater than any other financing method with which the machine might be bought. Therefore, in the evaluation of such a lease, the lessee must consider whether or not these additional financing costs are worthwhile in exchange for the reduction in risk provided by the cancellation option.

A final difference between the two types of lease which may be significant is the difference in accounting treatment. Finance leases should be recorded in the balance sheet as an asset and an obligation to pay future rentals. On the other hand, there is no requirement to capitalize operating leases in the same way: they are 'off balance sheet'. It has been suggested that the distinction is significant in that 'off balance sheet' finance does not affect any of the critical balance sheet or profitability ratios. Insofar as these ratios influence the potential providers of capital for the company, the use of finance leases as against other forms of long-term debt finance may affect the company's ability to raise new finance.

18
Overseas capital investments

Answer to problem 1

(a) *Calculations*

    (1) *Net revenues*
        Year 1: $5 \times 400 = 2,000 \times 0.7 = 1,400$
        Year 2: $5.5 \times 400 \times 1.15 = 2,530 \times 0.7 = 1,771$
        Year 3: $6 \times 400 \times 1.15^2 = 3,174 \times 0.7 = 2,221.8$
        Year 4: $6.5 \times 400 \times 1.15^3 = 3,954.275 \times 0.7 = 2,768$

    (2) *Parts cost*
        Year 1: $5 \quad \times 80 = 400$
        Year 2: $5.5 \times 80 = 440 \times 1.15 \quad = 506$
        Year 3: $6 \quad \times 80 = 480 \times 1.15^2 = 634.8$
        Year 4: $6.5 \times 80 = 520 \times 1.15^3 = 790.9$

    (3) *Depreciation*
$$\frac{4,000}{5 \text{ (years)}} = 800$$

    (4) *Tax charge*
        20% on accounting profits

    (5) *Royalties*
        (See calculations at reference 1)
        Year 1: $2,000 \times 0.15 = 300$
        Year 2: $2,530 \times 0.15 = 379.5$
        Year 3: $3,174 \times 0.15 = 476.1$
        Year 4: $3,954 \times 0.15 = 593.1$

    (6) *Incremental working capital requirements*
        (Additional (incremental))
        Year 1: $2,000 \quad \times 0.2 = 400$
        Year 2: $2,530 \quad \times 0.2 = 506 - 400 = 106$
        Year 3: $3,174 \quad \times 0.2 = 634.8 - 504 = 128.8$
        Year 4: $3,954.275 \times 0.2 = 790.9 - 634.8 = 156.1$
        (Assumed that the working capital is required at the start of
        each year.)

(7) *Capital outlay*
  (4,000 + 600 + 400) = 5,000 × 0.6 = 3,000

(8) *Parts contribution*
  Year 1: 400 × 0.4 = 160
  Year 2: 506 × 0.4 = 202.4
  Year 3: 634.8 × 0.4 = 253.92
  Year 4: 790.9 × 0.4 = 316.36

(9) *Dividends*
  60% of total dividends.

(10) *Share sale proceeds (m. Bandls)*
  After tax Year 4 profit (before royalties):

   348.58 + 593.1 = 941.68

  Capitalized value: 941.68 × 11 = 10,358.48
  60% capitalized value: 10,358.48 × 0.60 = 6,215.088

Taxable profits (m. Bandls)

Year	Calculation	1	2	3	4
Net revenues	(1)	1,400	1,771	2,221.8	2,768
Parts cost	(2)	(400)	(506)	(634.8)	(790.9)
Depreciation	(3)	(800)	(800)	(800)	(800)
Taxable profit		200	465	787	1,177.1
Tax charge	(4)	40	93	157.4	235.42

Accounting profit (m. Bandls)

Year		1	2	3	4
Net revenues		1,400	1,771	2,221.8	2,768
Parts cost		(400)	(506)	(634.8)	(790.9)
Depreciation		(800)	(800)	(800)	(800)
Royalties	(5)	(300)	(379.5)	(476.1)	(593.1)
Tax charge		(40)	(93)	(157.4)	(235.42)
Profit (loss)		(140)	(7.5)	153.5	348.58
Accumulated loss				(147.5)	
Available for dividend		–	–	6.0	348.58

Net cash flow (m. Bandls)

Year		1	2	3	4
Net revenues		1,400	1,771	2,221.8	2,766.4
Parts cost		(400)	(506)	(634.8)	(790.9)
Royalties		(300)	(379.5)	(476.1)	(593.1)
Tax payment		–	(40)	(93)	(157.4)
Dividends		–	–	(6.0)	(348.58)
Net cash flow		700	845.5	1,011.9	876.42
Working capital requirement	(6)	106	128.8	156.1	

There is sufficient free cash flow within the company to supply the incremental working capital requirements.

NPV analysis (m. Bandls)

Year	Calculation	0	1	2	3	4
Outlay	(7)	(3,000)				
Royalties			300	379.5	476.1	593.1
Parts contribution	(8)		160	202.4	253.92	316.36
Dividends	(9)				3.6	209.328
Share sale	(10)					6,215.088
		(3,000)	460	581.9	733.62	7,333.876
Exchange rate		÷500	÷550	÷605	÷666	÷732
£m.		(6.0)	0.836	0.962	1.101	9.991
Discount rate		×1	×0.8333	×0.6944	×0.5787	×0.4823
P.V. c/f		(6.0)	0.6966	0.6680	0.6371	4.8197

Net present value +£821,400

On the basis of these calculations and the estimates made, the proposed investment would appear to be worthwhile. It can be expected to yield a positive NPV of approximately £820,000.

(b) There are two basic decisions that have to be made in financing overseas investments. The first concerns how much of the finance is to be raised in the overseas country and how much is to be financed via the export of sterling. The second decision concerns the form of the exported finance: equity or debt.

The financing method chosen for overseas projects is important. The method chosen has an impact on the firm's exposure to translation risk and to country risk (and also to the risks surrounding the remittance of the project's net cash flows to the parent).

As far as translation risk is concerned, the more the project can be financed in the overseas currency, the greater is the degree of protection afforded the parent through the *matching* of overseas currency assets and liabilities. Assuming that 100% financing in the overseas currency is either not possible or not desirable, the standard advice is to finance the property assets required and the working capital with an overseas currency loan, and finance the project's non-property fixed assets with exported sterling.

The logic behind this advice is as follows. As stated previously, the matching principle will protect the parent from FX risk exposure on the property assets and working capital. In addition, the parent will also receive some (but *not* perfect) protection on the non-property fixed assets through the workings of the law of one price. (In other words, assuming that the non-property fixed assets are capable of being internationally traded, the value of those assets in terms of the overseas currency should rise to offset any weakness in the exchange rate.)

With the project under consideration, 5,000m Bandls are required, of which 4,000m are for non-property fixed assets. As only 3,000m Bandls are going to be financed through the export of sterling, this would suggest that the proposed financing method will result in Alcandro being reasonably well hedged against FX risk. However, the fact that equity rather than loan financing is being used does, to some extent, weaken the protection against translation risk exposure as the company will hold 60% of *all* the project's assets, and not just the non-property fixed assets.

Turning to the second factor of importance (country risk), obviously the 40% local equity financing will help to give Alcandro some protection against possible project nationalization without proper compensation. It may also help to reduce the risk of the host government changing in an adverse manner the fiscal regime under which the project is expected to operate.

At the same time, the all-equity financing method which has been chosen – plus the other conditions applied – does mean that Alcandro is relying upon just three routes by which to remit the project's net cash flow back to the UK: dividends, royalty payments and transfer prices, plus the subsequent share sale. If the exported sterling was in the form of loans, some of the project's net cash flow could have been remitted back in the form of interest payments, which are often seen as being much less politically sensitive than are dividend payments. Hence such a channel for net cash flow remittance is much less likely to suffer from government-imposed restrictions than are dividend payments. Additionally, it may well be argued that the subsequent loan repayment would also be at less risk of FX restrictions than would the equity sale proceeds.

Finally, if some of the finance could have been provided via a loan raised from a large international bank, this might have given Alcandro some additional protection against severe manifestations of country risk. The host government might well hesitate before taking actions which might cause the project to default on its loans, when the lending institution was also involved in sovereign lending.

Answer to problem 2

(a) *Discount rate*
Given:

$$\beta_A = \frac{\sigma_A \cdot \rho_{A,M}}{\sigma_M}$$

then

$$\beta_{Subsidiary} = \frac{\sigma_{Subsidiary} \cdot \rho_{Subsidiary, Market}}{\sigma_{Market}}$$

$$\beta_{Subsidiary} = \frac{0.65 \times 0.885}{0.48} = \underline{1.2 \text{ approx}}$$

Using CAPM:

$$E[r_{\text{Subsidiary}}] = r_f + (E[r_{\text{Market}}] - r_f)\beta_{\text{Subsidiary}}$$
$$E[r_{\text{Subsidiary}}] = 8\% + [13\% - 8\%] \times 1.2 = \underline{\underline{14\%}}$$

Writing down allowances

Assuming that the capital expenditure is incurred on the first day of the company's accounting year:

£m   £m

15   × 0.25 = 3.75 × 0.35 = 1.312 Year 2 ⎫
   3.75 |
11.25 × 0.25 = 2.81 × 0.35 = 0.984 Year 3 |
   2.81   ⎬ Writing down
 8.44 × 0.25 = 2.11 × 0.35 = 0.739 Year 4 | allowance
   2.11 |
 6.33 × 0.25 = 1.58 × 0.35 = 0.553 Year 5 ⎭
   1.58
 4.75 − 10   = (5.25)× 0.35 = (1.837) Year 6 Balancing charge

Contribution/gallon

£300 − £140	= £160/gal.	Year 1
£160(1.04)	= £166.4/gal.	Year 2
£166.4(1.03)	= £171.39/gal.	Year 3
£171.39(1.03)	= £176.53/gal.	Year 4
£176.53(1.04)	= £183.59/gal.	Year 5

Annual contribution

Year	Contrib/gal.	× Sales	=	£m
1	£160	× 20,000	=	3.2
2	166.4	× 50,000	=	8.32
3	171.39	× 50,000	=	8.57
4	176.53	× 50,000	=	8.827
5	183.59	× 50,000	=	9.18

Annual fixed costs

Year		£m
1	2	= 2
2	2(1.04)	= 2.08
3	2.08(1.03)	= 2.142
4	2.142(1.03)	= 2.206
5	2.206(1.04)	= 2.294

Exchange rates

$$
\begin{aligned}
\text{Spot} &= 1.5500 \\
\text{Year 1} &= 1.4725 \\
\text{Year 2: } 1.4725\,(1 - 0.05) &= 1.3989 \\
\text{Year 3: } 1.3989\,(1 - 0.05) &= 1.3289 \\
\text{Year 4: } 1.3289\,(1 - 0.05) &= 1.2625 \\
\text{Year 5: } 1.2625\,(1 - 0.05) &= 1.1994
\end{aligned}
$$

Royalty payments

Year	Sales			$m.	÷	Exchange Rate		£m.
1	20,000	×	$50	= 1.0	÷	1.4725	=	0.679
2	50,000	×	$50	= 2.5	÷	1.3989	=	1.787
3	50,000	×	$50	= 2.5	÷	1.3289	=	1.881
4	50,000	×	$50	= 2.5	÷	1.2625	=	1.980
5	50,000	×	$50	= 2.5	÷	1.1994	=	2.084

Tax charges (£m)

Year	Contrib.	− Fixed costs	− Royalties	=	Taxable c/f	×	Tax rate	=	Tax charge	Tax timing
1	3.2	− 2	− 0.679	=	0.521	×	0.35	=	0.182	2
2	8.32	− 2.08	− 1.787	=	4.453	×	0.35	=	1.558	3
3	8.57	− 2.142	− 1.881	=	4.547	×	0.35	=	1.591	4
4	8.827	− 2.206	− 1.980	=	4.641	×	0.35	=	1.624	5
5	9.18	− 2.294	− 2.084	=	4.802	×	0.35	=	1.681	6

Project cash flows (£ million)

	0	1	2	3	4	5	6
Outlay	−15						
Grant	+3						
Scrap						+10	
WDA			+1.312	+0.984	+0.739	+0.553	−1.837
Contribution		+3.2	+8.32	+8.57	+8.827	+9.18	
Fixed costs		−2	−2.08	−2.142	−2.206	−2.294	
Tax charge			−0.182	−1.558	−1.591	−1.624	−1.681
Net cash flow	−12	+1.2	+7.37	+5.854	+5.769	+15.815	−3.518
Discount factor	1	0.8772	0.7695	0.6750	0.5921	0.5194	0.4556
P.V. c/f	−12	+1.053	+5.671	+3.951	+3.416	+8.214	−1.603

NPV of proposed UK subsidiary: +£8.702 million.

The royalty cash flow has been excluded from this calculation (but not the impact of the royalty payments on the corporate tax charge) because it should be included as part of the project's net cash flow available for remittance back to the US parent.

In US dollar terms, the project could be expected to have a positive NPV of: £8.702m × 1.55 = $13.488 million.

In addition, there is a further opportunity benefit arising out of the project. At present the UK market is supplied from the US where there is no spare production capacity. The UK project will make some spare production capacity become available in the US, which will allow the company to exploit the Scandinavian market and so generate an after-tax net cash flow of £1.5m.

On the assumption that the Scandinavian market 'project' has the same risk as the UK project, then the interest rate parity theorem could be used to estimate a suitable discount rate to apply to these incremental after-tax US$ cash flows:

$$\frac{1 + \$ \text{ discount rate}}{1 + £ \text{ discount rate}} = \frac{12\text{mth Forward } \$/£}{\text{Spot } \$/£}$$

$$\frac{1 + \$ \text{ discount rate}}{1 + 0.14} = \frac{1.4725}{1.5500}$$

$$\$ \text{ discount rate} = \frac{1.14 \times 1.4725}{1.5500} - 1 = \underline{0.083 \text{ or } 8.3\%}$$

Thus the present value of the Scandinavian market could be estimated as:

$$\frac{\$1.5\text{m}}{0.083} = \underline{\underline{\$18.07\text{m PV}}}$$

(b)　Investment in any overseas project is likely to expose the parent company to FX translation risk. In this particular case Blue Grass Distillery Inc would have sterling assets and, if it finances the project by exporting dollars, dollar liabilities.

The easiest way to avoid this risk is to match the overseas currency assets with a liability in that same currency. However, such a perfect hedge may not be legally possible (the project's host country might insist that at least some of the finance should be exported by the parent) or may not be seen to be advisable from a public relations viewpoint.

In such circumstances, the standard advice is that a project's non-property fixed assets should be financed with sterling, while the property fixed assets, together with the working capital, should be financed in the currency of the host country. The reasoning behind this advice is that the company can hedge part of its foreign exchange risk through matching assets and liabilities in the same currency, while at the same time it gets some protection from foreign exchange risk on its unmatched assets through the workings of the Law of One Price. The reason why the non-property fixed assets are left unmatched is that they are the most likely assets to react to the Law of One Price. Therefore if sterling depreciates against the US dollar (as it is expected to do) it might be reasonable to assume that the sterling worth of the non-property fixed assets may rise in order to counteract the reduced worth of sterling, assuming that those assets are capable of being traded internationally.

Answer to problem 3

(a) *Base-case present value*

Base-case discount rate (£ terms)

$$\beta_{assets} = 1.40 \times \frac{4}{4 + 1(1 - 0.35)} = 1.20$$

Base-Case discount rate $= 9\% + [9.17\% \times 1.20] = \underline{20\%}$

A$ project tax charge (A$m)

Years		1 – 4
	Revenue	18
–	Operation costs	(5)
–	Depreciation	(3.75)
=	Taxable profit	9.25
	Tax charge	4.625

A$ project cash flows (A$m)

Year	0	1	2	3	4
Capital equipment	(15)				
Working capital	(5)				5
Revenues		18	18	18	18
Costs		(5)	(5)	(5)	(5)
Taxation		(4.625)	(4.625)	(4.625)	(4.625)
Net cash flow	(20)	8.375	8.375	8.375	13.375

£m base-case present value calculation

Year	A$m	÷	Exchange rate	=	£m	×	20% discount rate	=	£m PV cash flows
0	(20)	÷	2	=	(10)	×	1	=	(10)
1	8.375	÷	$2(1.10)^1$	=	3.807	×	0.833	=	3.171
2	8.375	÷	$2(1.10)^2$	=	3.461	×	0.694	=	2.402
3	8.375	÷	$2(1.10)^3$	=	3.146	×	0.579	=	1.821
4	13.375	÷	$2(1.10)^4$	=	4.568	×	0.482	=	2.202
					Base case PV			=	(£404m)

PV of financing side-effects

PV of tax shield

$$£5m \times 0.10 \quad = £500,000 = \text{Annual interest}$$
$$£500,000 \times 0.35 = £175,000 = \text{Annual tax relief}$$

PV of tax relief: $175,000 \ A_{\overline{4}|0.10} = £554,750$

PV of issue costs

$$£5m \times 0.025 \times (1 - 0.35) = (£81,250)$$

Adjusted present value

	£m
Base-case PV	(0.404)
PV Tax shield	0.555
PV issue costs	(0.081)
Adjusted present value	£0.07m or +£70,000 approx.

Therefore, the project should be accepted.

(b)   The company's proposed financing plans for the Australian project can be criticized on the basis that they have not taken the opportunity to arrange them so as to help limit exposure to foreign exchange risk.

By having a long-lived Australian dollar (A$) asset the company is exposing itself to both foreign exchange translation and transaction risk. This risk can be reduced by matching the A$ assets as closely as possible to an A$ liability.

The standard advice – given on the assumption that the company will have to finance some part of its overseas project by exporting sterling – is that the project's non-property fixed assets should be financed with sterling, while the property fixed assets, together with the working capital, should be financed in the currency of the host country. The reasoning behind this advice is that the company can hedge part of its foreign exchange risk through matching assets and liabilities in the same currency, while at the same time it gets some protection from foreign exchange risk on its unmatched assets through the workings of the law of one price. The reason why the non-property fixed assets are left unmatched is that they are the most likely assets to react to the law of one price. Therefore if the A$ depreciates against sterling (as it is expected to do) it might be reasonable to assume that the A$ worth of the non-property fixed assets may rise in order to counteract the reduced worth of the A$, assuming that those assets are capable of being traded internationally.

Answer to problem 4

(a) *Calculations*

Revenues (Cm)

Year	1	2	3	4	5	6
Volume	500	510	520	530	540	550
Price	3	3.3	3.6	4.0	4.4	4.8
Revenues	1500	1683	1872	2120	2376	2640

Components (Cm)

Year	1	2	3	4	5	6
Volume	500	510	520	530	540	550
	×	×	×	×	×	×
£ cost per unit	5000	5300	5600	6000	6300	6700
	×	×	×	×	×	×
Exchange rate	156	162	169	175	182	190
Crolls (m)	390	437.9	492.1	556.5	619.2	700.2

Sale proceeds (Cm)

$6 \times (447.6 - 179) = 1611.6$

Tax charge (Cm)

Year	1	2	3	4	5	6
Revenues	1500	1683	1872	2120	2376	2640
Components	(390)	(437.9)	(492.1)	(556.1)	(619.2)	(700.2)
Production costs	(675)	(757.4)	(842.4)	(954)	(1069.2)	(1188)
Net revenues	435	487.7	537.5	609.9	687.6	751.8
Depreciation	(240)	(240)	(240)	(240)	(240)	–
Taxed profit	195	247.7	297.5	369.9	447.6	751.8
Tax at 40%	(78)	(99.1)	(119)	(147.8)	(179)	(300.7)

NPV analysis for investors in Heina

Year	0	1	2	3	4	5	6
Equipment	(1200)						
Working capital	(160)	10	(18.3)	(18.9)	(24.8)	(25.6)	237.6
Net revenues		435	487.7	537.5	609.9	687.6	751.8
Tax		(78)	(99.1)	(119)	(147.8)	(179)	(300.7)
Net cash flow	(1360)	367	370.3	399.6	436.9	483	688.7
20% discount rate		0.8333	0.6944	0.5787	0.4823	0.4019	0.3349
P.V. cash flow	(1360)	305.8	257.1	231.2	210.7	194.1	230.6

NPV: + C 69.5m.

Therefore the project is acceptable.

(b)

Year	0	1	2	3	4	5
Net cash flow	(1360)	367	370.3	399.6	436.9	483
Sale proceeds						1611.6
Tax charge						(483.5)
Cm cash flow	(1360)	367	370.3	399.6	436.9	1611.1
C/£	150	156	162	169	175	182
£m cash flow	(9.067)	2.353	2.286	2.364	2.497	8.852
25% discount rate		0.8000	0.6400	0.5120	0.4096	0.3277
£ PV c/f	(9.067)	1.882	1.463	1.210	1.023	2.901

NPV: −£0.588m.

Therefore the project is *not* acceptable from the viewpoint of Eibl plc and its UK investors.

(c) Eibl proposes to provide an initial cash injection followed by continuing support of the subsidiary's working capital requirements. It will also provide components at cost and thus will be generated within Heina and thus liable to that country's business tax rate.

Given that, on the basis of calculations in (b) above, the venture seems unacceptable for Eibl's shareholders, there appear to be two factors that could be considered:
(i)   alternative financing methods for the initial and continuing cash injections;
(ii)   supplying components at a cost plus price thus generating some profit for Eibl itself rather than the Heina subsidiary.
In order to limit the discussion there are certain points that will not be considered in detail.
(i)   All data are estimated with sufficient accuracy. We can therefore concentrate on financing rather than investment problems.
(ii)   The valuation of the sale price of the subsidiary is appropriate.
(iii) The tax rates in Heina will stay constant over the period.

Alternative financing methods
Eibl has two options:
(i)   It may export the required funds from the UK.
(ii)   It may attempt to raise funds in the currency in which the investment is to be made either through equity or debt finance. In many countries which do not have highly-developed capital markets this can prove difficult and it is rarely possible to raise all necessary funds in this way.
In practice most direct foreign investment is financed by foreign currency borrowing.

Exporting funds from the UK is the method proposed by Eibl. The success of this depends on the extent to which the Heina-based assets will hold their sterling value as the Croll depreciates. If they think the value will hold up well then the sterling input may be appropriate. It could however consider issuing sterling debt to finance the initial investment rather than using its own cash reserves. The continuing working capital injections are more worrying as they open Eibl to currency risk on the operations rather than the assets. Eibl is advised to consider local borrowing for short-term capital requirements.

If Eibl raises funds within Heina it will reduce its exposure to currency risk but will need to consider any problems that may be associated with the remittance of funds from the subsidiary to the parent company. In some circumstances remittances by some combination of interest, dividends, royalty payments and management fees may prove to be more reliable than dividend payments.

Some combination of direct and local financing may be more appropriate than that proposed by Eibl.

Alternative pricing of components
Eibl intends supplying components at cost. This decision could be based on a variety of factors for example:

(i)   a desire to identify Heina as a local profit centre and thus improve management performance and allow effective management assessment;
(ii)   the achievement of a profit maximizing level of output for Eibl (UK) plc;
(iii) the lack of alternative uses for the components within the UK or other markets;
(iv)   existing tax positions and rates in both UK and Heina support the contention that profits should be made in Heina.

Obviously with limited information it is difficult to assess the decision made by Heina to transfer components at cost. It could however be possible that the project may be acceptable from the UK investors' viewpoint if this decision were reconsidered particularly in relation to relative rates of tax.

19
The dividend decision

Answer to problem 1

(a) (i) Cum-dividend price after declaration of £150,000 dividend
= 140p.

The total value of Pulini plc will be £1.4m.

(ii) The current price reflects the expected dividend of £150,000.
The share price should increase by the NPV of the contract.

$$K_E = \frac{\text{dividend}}{\text{Ex-div value}} = \frac{15}{125} = 12\%$$

$$\text{NPV} = £80,000 + \frac{£80,000}{0.12} - \frac{£22,400}{0.12} = +£560,000$$

Share price should increase by £560,000 ÷ 1m. = 56p

Revised cum-dividend price = 196p
Revised total value = £1.96m

(iii) By using the £80,000 revenue from the project Pulini can
increase its current dividend from 15p to 23p per share. The
way in which the market responds to this will depend upon
whether it is efficient in the semi-strong or strong form.

(1) Semi-strong

The revised price will depend upon whether the market supposes that the increased dividend is a one-off
payment for this year only, or, based on Pulini's past
record of constant dividends, anticipates the increased
dividend to continue indefinitely.

'one-off'   Cum-div price = 140p + 8p = 148p
Total value £1.48m

130

$$\text{continuing} \quad 23p + \frac{23p}{0.12} = 215p$$

Total value £2.15m

(2) Strong form

If the market is efficient in the strong form it will learn of the project and the share price will adjust to 196p as calculated in part (ii) above.

(b) In theory, dividends are a passive residual in the context of financial decision making. As positive net present value of investment projects accrues to shareholders it must necessarily be the company's aim to enter into all projects giving positive net present value even if this entails reductions in dividends below previously existing levels. Funds not required for investment will be paid out as dividends. For these ideas to be valid there must be perfect information about company activities available to shareholders, who must understand and believe the information. They will then accept any reduction in dividend as being in their own interest and the share price will in fact rise to reflect this improvement in the value of the company.

In the short term at least, the reduction of dividends to finance beneficial investment would in theory substitute a capital gain for dividends. Shareholders must be prepared to accept this distribution. They will do so only if they can borrow at the same rate as the company (and repay later out of a future enhanced dividend) or if they can realize the capital gain to obtain cash in substitution for the dividend. These will only be adequate substitutes if there are no transaction costs or distorting taxes.

If the conditions necessary to uphold the 'dividend irrelevancy theory' were met in practice then dividends would truly be a residual and not a determining factor in the valuation of a company. However, in reality, they do not hold well and it is necessary to examine those aspects of dividend policy which may in practice affect a company's market value.

It is information which determines share price and one of the principal pieces of objective information available to investors to assist them in pricing shares is the level of dividend. Whilst published accounts and reported earnings are extremely useful, they are both historical, indicating what the company has done rather than what it is doing or will do. Dividends are, by contrast, an indicator of the current state of the company and its future prospects. The amount of, and trends in, dividends are thus strongly reacted to by the market. This is strikingly illustrated by the different reactions to reduced dividends in theory and practice. In theory this could well herald further beneficial investment and increased company value whereas in practice it is likely to be seen as evidence of severe difficulties and the share price is likely to drop.

Even if the management set out clearly their intentions for the use of funds, it is possible that the message will not be fully understood, or may be treated with scepticism. In view of these practical realities, company management are likely to pursue a policy of dividend stability and, where possible, steady growth at a prudent rate. Above all shareholders require a consistent policy. Where this is possible uncertainty, and hence risk, is reduced. The rate of return required by investors may therefore be adjusted downwards leading to higher market capitalization.

In summary, investors are not indifferent between current dividends and the retention of earnings with the prospect of future dividends, capital gains, or both. They prefer the resolution of uncertainty and are willing to pay a higher price or a share that pays a greater current dividend, all other things being equal.

(c) The factors which will influence company management's dividend policy relate essentially to prudence, company funding requirements and regard for individual shareholders' requirements.

With regard to prudence, it might well be that whilst a company makes good profits, a significant proportion of these may not be realized in cash terms and it is therefore not possible to pay substantial dividends without placing strains on the company's liquidity. Dividends must be budgeted for as an integral part of the cash flow forecast and where necessary further funds obtained for the purpose of dividend payments. The alternative to this is a more restrained payout policy.

Company management will also have regard to future funding requirements. Use of retained earnings is one of the simplest and cheapest ways of obtaining finance for expansion, and it is therefore quite attractive to management to pursue a relatively low payout policy in order to retain funds for expansion. The company's access to capital markets will also play a large part in the decision on retention policy. A company with ready access to capital markets may in practice prefer a higher payout policy coupled with regular rights issues rather than keep dividends deliberately low to provide a large pool of retained earnings. Smaller companies cannot count on this advantage and therefore in practice will seek funding largely from retained earnings.

In financial management it is generally assumed that the objective of company management is to follow a policy of maximizing the wealth of shareholders. To this end dividend policy is of vital importance. Clearly a high retentions policy is commensurate with high capital growth in share value whilst high payouts will benefit shareholders who require high income. Whilst in a perfect capital market with no taxes this differentiation of policy would be irrelevant, in actuality the tax position of shareholders will significantly influence their accumulation of wealth through shareholdings. Whilst in large companies researching shareholders' preferences and setting policy accordingly might be impracticable, this will not necessarily be so in small companies where tax considerations may well play an extremely important part in setting dividend policy.

It should not be forgotten that dividends can only be paid regularly where the company is inherently profitable and hence management must examine profitability in setting dividend policy, and in particular the stability of earnings. Where earnings are very stable the company will be less at risk in following a high percentage payout policy than if earnings are extremely volatile. Dividend cuts are usually anathema to company management as the market is likely to consider that this presages bad news, with consequent disastrous effects on share price. Hence companies with volatile earnings are unlikely to risk dividend cuts by pursuing a high payout policy. Indeed good dividend policy is to pursue the ideals of stability and consistency. Variable dividends are uncertain dividends, giving rise to an increased risk perception in shareholders. This feeds through into a higher required return and hence lower market capitalization, defeating the company aim of shareholder wealth maximization.

While the conventional models assume the objective of maximization of shareholder wealth this may not be the objective being pursued by particular companies. It may be that corporate managers are pursuing alternative objectives such as sales maximization, market share maximization or the maximization of managerial discretion subject to the constraint of providing an acceptable return to investors. Alternatively managers may not be maximizing at all but may be 'satisficing', i.e. pursuing a battery of parallel objectives. In such circumstances they will need to modify their dividend policies to suit the objectives they are pursuing. In any event they will need to know what constitutes an acceptable return to their investors and this in turn requires a knowledge of what can be earned on similar risk investments elsewhere, i.e. the opportunity cost of capital.

Finally it cannot be forgotten that there are legal requirements governing dividend payments and company management must have regard to the legal definitions of distributable profits.

Answer to problem 2

In terms of shareholder wealth, dividends obviously play a crucial role. The dividend valuation model, for instance, indicates that the market value of a company's shares represents the discounted sum of the future expected dividend stream that will accrue. However, on a year-by-year basis, shareholders receive their return in two forms: the capital gain (or loss) arising from share price appreciation (or depreciation) and the dividend.

The company's management can determine how the shareholders' total annual return on equity is 'packaged' through the dividend policy they pursue. If the management follow a policy of paying out a high level of dividends and retaining a low proportion of earnings, then most of the return can be expected in the form of dividends, with very little capital gain. Conversely, a management which retains a high proportion of earnings – and so only pays out a low level of dividends – will cause most of the annual return to be in the form of capital gains. (The re-invested earnings will, it is assumed, allow higher dividend payments in future years. It is the present value of these increased dividends that causes the share price to rise, bringing about a capital gain.)

In a perfect capital market world of no taxes and no transaction costs, shareholders would be indifferent as to how their own return on equity is packaged between dividends and capital gains. Thus dividend policy would be irrelevant – it would not affect shareholder wealth. This is, effectively, the M and M dividend irrelevancy argument and it is clearly the hypothesis which the finance director of Chartwell Leasing remembers from his MBA course.

However, in the real world both taxes and transaction costs exist and so the dividend decision does become important as it can affect shareholder wealth. The existence of transaction costs mean that investors will incur these costs if they wish to realize that part of their annual return received in the form of a capital gain. Thus, on this basis, dividends are likely to be preferred to capital gains.

Taxation brings additional complications. Tax exempt investors (such as pension funds) can reclaim the ACT paid on dividends, but there is no corresponding tax reclaim on capital gains. Therefore such investors would strongly prefer dividends rather than capital gains. (In addition, there is another reason. Pension funds can legally only pay pensions out of revenue account, not out of capital account and so capital gains could not be used to pay their annual pension commitments.)

From a tax point of view, the basic rate taxpayer is likely to be indifferent between dividend and capital gain income. No further tax liability is due on dividends (basic rate tax already being imputed as being paid) and, given CGT allowances, it is unlikely that they would have any CGT liability on their capital gains.

In contrast there is a preference for capital gains by the shareholder who pays personal tax at a higher rate. For such a shareholder the tax rate on capital gains is likely to be significantly less than that on dividend income (because of CGT allowances). Furthermore, such a shareholder can choose when is the most tax-efficient time to take the capital gains, whilst he has got to accept the dividend tax liability as soon as the dividend is paid.

Therefore, given the fact that transaction costs and taxes exist in the real world, it would appear that the best course of action that companies can take regarding dividend policy is to follow a consistent policy (either high or low dividends), so as to attract to them a group of shareholders whose own personal tax position suits that particular dividend policy. In this respect the chairman's comment would appear to be sensible. The treasurer's idea on dividend policy, that the dividend decision should be a residual of the investment decision, would be likely to lead to a highly variable dividend from one year to another and so would tend to go against the 'clientele' argument.

A further reason against the treasurer's idea concerns the 'signalling effect' of dividends (sometimes referred to as the information content of dividends). It is often believed that the stock market reads signals or imputes information about the company's future performance in the dividend decision. If this is so, then a policy of paying out a highly variable level of dividends from year to year that would result from treating the dividend decision as a residual of the investment decision, would lead to confusing and misleading signals being given to the stock market.

Finally, it should be pointed out that great uncertainty still exists about the identification of a 'proper' dividend policy and its effect on shareholder wealth. The 'information content' argument appears to go against the idea – and evidence – of a semi-strong efficient stock market. While the empirical evidence on the 'clientele effect' is mixed and some would argue that, if it were to exist, then it would open up arbitrage opportunities if there were not a balance between the clientele wanting high dividends and those wanting high capital gains.

Answer to problem 3

(a)   Net present value to Charles Pooter (Contractors) plc

$$\text{NPV} = -3,000 + 800(1.04) + 1,000(1.04)^{-2} + 1,700(1.04)^{-3}$$
$$= -3,000 + 769 + 925 + 1,511 = \underline{+£205}$$

(b)   (i)   Lupin is satisfied (as stated in the question). Charles can borrow one half of the present value of the cash inflows from the project (i.e. he can borrow the present value of the dividends he expects to receive):

Charles can borrow ($\frac{1}{2}$ × £3,205) £1,602 at 4% (and go on cruise)	
Interest Year 1 at 4%	64
	1,666
Repay end Year 1 ($\frac{1}{2}$ × £800)	400
	1,266
Interest Year 2 at 4%	51
	1,317
Repay end Year 2 ($\frac{1}{2}$ × £1,000)	500
	817
Interest Year 3 at 4%	33
	850
Repay end Year 3 ($\frac{1}{2}$ × £1,700)	850

By borrowing, and using his dividends to repay the loan, Charles is £102 better off if the project is accepted than if it is rejected. So the company is acting in the best interests of both shareholders by accepting the project.

(ii)   Lupin is still satisfied (as stated in the question). The present value of Charles's dividends at 10% is:

$$400(1.10)^{-1} + 500(1.10)^{-2} + 850(1.10)^{-3}$$

$$= 400(0.9091) + 500(0.8264) + 850(0.7513) = £1,415$$

which is the maximum amount he could borrow and repay out of his share of the project dividends. He would be better off with an immediate dividend of £1,500. So the company is not acting in the best interests of both shareholders.

(c)   The above analysis suggests that the net present value rule results in correct investment decisions provided that all shareholders have the same 'cost of capital' as the company, even if their consumption preferences vary. Any shareholder can adjust his dividend receipts to fit his desired consumption pattern by lending or borrowing. (b)(ii) suggests that the net present value rule needs to be applied cautiously where shareholders' costs of capital differ from the company's (e.g. where capital markets are imperfect). In this case it may not be possible for shareholders to adjust their consumption patterns by lending or borrowing without incurring an interest cost different from the company's.